PENNSYLVANIA

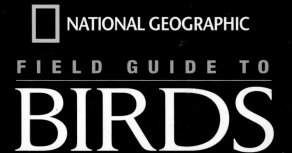

NATIONAL GEOGRAPHIC

FIELD GUIDE TO
BIRDS

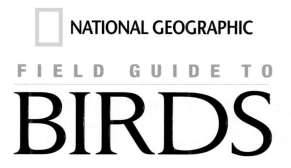

PENNSYLVANIA

NATIONAL GEOGRAPHIC

FIELD GUIDE TO

BIRDS

Edited by JONATHAN ALDERFER

National Geographic
Washington, D.C.

Introduction

All the birds in this book are reasonably easy to find in Pennsylvania. For some species, this is true only if you know where, when, and how to look for them. You might search unsuccessfully for a Snow Goose in the western counties, but thousands visit Middle Creek Wildlife Management Area every March. A Broad-winged Hawk might be hard to find in its woodland breeding haunts, but large numbers migrate over Hawk Mountain Sanctuary in September. Gorgeous Blackburnian Warblers are not widespread nesters, but for a good chance of seeing one, scan tall conifers in the Allegheny National Forest in June. Finding a Barn Owl may be the biggest challenge, but diligent detective work should reward you.

Pennsylvania abounds in outstanding bird-finding locations, which birders call "hot spots" for their great numbers and variety of species. At opposite corners of the state, Presque Isle State Park and John Heinz National Wildlife Refuge famously attract multitudes of migratory land and water birds. Appalachian mountaintops such as the Kittatinny Ridge are spectacular places to watch migrating hawks and eagles. Forests, fields, streams, and shrubby patches in 117 state parks are a summer home to 28 breeding warbler species. Charming farm-lands and vast surface-mine reclamation areas offer exciting grassland specialties, some of them quite rare. Surprisingly, the state's three largest cities are the easiest places to see rare Peregrine Falcons year-round.

About 200 bird species nest in Pennsylvania. Add migrants, winterers, and accidental visitors, and the state's official list exceeds 400 species. At many hot spots during spring and autumn, it is customary to see more than 100 species on a single day. Good birding!

Paul Hess
Past Chairman
Pennsylvania Ornithological Records Committee

frontispiece: Black-throated Green Warbler
Photo by Bob Steele

CONTENTS

8   ABOUT THIS BOOK
9   HOW TO USE THIS BOOK

15 GEESE, SWANS, DUCKS
45 PHEASANTS, GROUSE, TURKEYS
51 LOONS
53 GREBES
55 CORMORANTS
57 HERONS, EGRETS
63 VULTURES
65 HAWKS, EAGLES
79 FALCONS
83 COOTS, GALLINULES
85 PLOVERS
87 SANDPIPERS
95 GULLS, TERNS
103 PIGEONS, DOVES
107 CUCKOOS
109 OWLS
115 NIGHTHAWKS
117 SWIFTS
119 HUMMINGBIRDS
121 KINGFISHERS
123 WOODPECKERS
133 TYRANT FLYCATCHERS
139 VIREOS
145 JAYS, CROWS, RAVENS

151 LARKS
153 SWALLOWS
161 CHICKADEES, TITMICE
165 NUTHATCHES
167 CREEPERS
169 WRENS
173 KINGLETS
175 GNATCATCHERS
177 THRUSHES
185 MOCKINGBIRDS, THRASHERS
191 STARLINGS
193 WAXINGS
195 WOOD-WARBLERS
223 TANAGERS
225 NEW WORLD SPARROWS
239 CARDINALS, GROSBEAKS, BUNTINGS
245 BLACKBIRDS, ORIOLES
257 FINCHES
261 OLD WORLD SPARROWS

262 COLOR INDEX
266 ALPHABETICAL INDEX
270 ACKNOWLEDGMENTS, CREDITS

SELECTED BIRDING SITES OF
PENNSYLVANIA

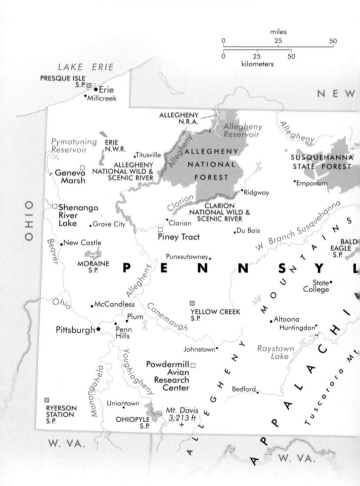

miles
0   25   50

0   25   50
kilometers

LAKE ERIE

NEW

PRESQUE ISLE
S.P.
• Erie
• Millcreek

ALLEGHENY
N.R.A.

Allegheny
Reservoir

Allegheny

SUSQUEHANNA
STATE FOREST

Pymatuning
Reservoir

ERIE
N.W.R.

• Titusville

Allegheny

ALLEGHENY
NATIONAL
FOREST

• Emporium

ALLEGHENY
NATIONAL WILD &
SCENIC RIVER

• Geneva
Marsh

Clarion

• Ridgway

□ Shenango
River
Lake

• Grove City

CLARION
NATIONAL WILD &
SCENIC RIVER

□ Clarion

• Du Bois

OHIO

Beaver

• New Castle

Piney Tract

P E N N S Y L
Punxsutawney •

W. Branch Susquehanna

BALD
EAGLE
S.P.

MORAINE
S.P.

Allegheny

M
o
u
n
t
a
i
n
s

State
College

Ohio

• McCandless

Conemaugh

□ YELLOW CREEK
S.P.

• Altoona
Huntingdon •

A
P
P
A
L
A
C
H
I
A

Pittsburgh

Plum •
Penn
Hills

Raystown
Lake

Johnstown •

Monongahela

Youghiogheny

Powdermill
Avian
Research
Center □

• Bedford

□ RYERSON
STATION
S.P.

• Uniontown

OHIOPYLE
S.P.

Mt. Davis
3,213 ft
+

A
L
L
E
G
H
E
N
Y

M
t
s

Tuscarora Mt

W. VA.

W. VA.

MAP KEY

National Park, N.P.
National Historical Park, N.H.P.
National Military Park, N.M.P.
National Recreation Area, N.R.A.

National Forest, N.F.
State Forest

National Wildlife Refuge, N.W.R.

State Park, S.P.
Wildlife Management Area, W.M.A.

State boundary
Trail
National wild & scenic river

↗ Dam
⊛ State capital
◻ Point of interest

YORK

Tioga

Pine Cr. Creek Gorge

Wellsboro

MOUNTAINS

Susquehanna

WORLDS END
S.P.

Williamsport

RICKETTS GLEN
S.P.

Wilkes-Barre

Scranton

Carbondale

UPPER DELAWARE
NATIONAL SCENIC
AND RECREATIONAL
RIVER

Delaware

Lake
Wallenpaupack

Lehigh

Pocono Mts.

DELAWARE
WATER GAP
NATIONAL
RECREATION
AREA

VANIA

BELTZVILLE
S.P.

TRAIL

Kittatinny Mts.

NEW
JERSEY

Juniata

Hawk Mt.
Sanctuary

APPALACHIAN

NATIONAL SCENIC

Blue Mountain

Ontelaunee

Allentown

Bethlehem

Easton

LOWER DELAWARE
NATIONAL WILD &
SCENIC RIVER

Quakertown

NOCKAMIXON
S.P.

Reading

Schuylkill

Green Lane
Reservoir

Levittown

Waggoners
Gap

Mechanicsburg

Harrisburg

MIDDLE CREEK
W.M.A.

Three
Mile
Island

York

Susquehanna

Lancaster

MARSH CREEK
S.P.

VALLEY FORGE N.H.P.

Norristown

Upper
Darby

Delaware

JOHN HEINZ N.W.R.

Chester

Philadelphia

ttysburg

GETTYSBURG
N.M.P.

Mason-Dixon
Line

DEL.

WHITE CLAY CR.
NATIONAL WILD &
SCENIC RIVER

MARYLAND

About this Book

Looking at Birds

What do the artist and the nature lover share? A passion for being attuned to the world and all of its complexity, via the senses. Every time you go out into the natural world, or even view it through a window, you have another opportunity to see what is there. And the more you know what you are looking at, the more you see.

Even if you are not yet a committed birder, it makes sense to take a field guide with you when you go out for a walk or a hike. Looking for and identifying birds will sharpen and heighten your perceptions, and intensify your experience. And you'll find that you notice everything else more acutely—the terrain, the season, the weather, the plant life, other animal life.

Birds are beautiful, complex animals that live everywhere around us in our towns and cities and in distant places we dream of visiting. Here in North America more than 900 species have been recorded—from abundant commoners to the rare and exotic. A comprehensive field reference like the *National Geographic Field Guide to the Birds of North America* is essential for understanding that big picture. If you are taking a spring walk in the Poconos, however, you may want something simpler: a guide to the birds you are most likely to see, which slips easily into a pocket.

This photographic guide is designed to provide an introduction to the common birds—and some of the specialty birds—you might encounter in Pennsylvania: how to identify them, how they behave, and where to find them, with specific locations.

Discovery, observation, and identification of birds is exciting, whether you are novice or expert. I know that every time I go out to look at birds, I see more clearly and have a greater appreciation for the natural world and my own place in it.

JONATHAN ALDERFER
Editor

National Geographic Field Guide to Birds: Pennsylvania is designed to help beginning and practiced birders alike identify birds in the field and introduce them to the region's varied birdlife. The book is organized by bird families, following the order in the *Check-list of North American Birds,* by the American Ornithologists' Union. Families share structural characteristics, and by learning these shared characteristics early, birders can establish a basis for a lifetime of identifying birds and related family members with great accuracy—sometimes merely at a glance. (For quick reference in the field, use the color and alphabetical indexes at the back of this book.)

A family may have one member or dozens of members, or species. In this book each family is identified by its common name in English along the right-hand border of each spread. Each species is also identified in English, with its Latin genus and species—its scientific name—found directly underneath. One species is featured in each entry.

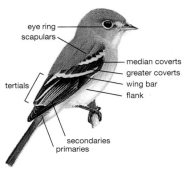

eye ring
scapulars
median coverts
greater coverts
wing bar
flank
tertials
secondaries
primaries

Least Flycatcher

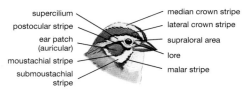

supercilium
postocular stripe
ear patch (auricular)
moustachial stripe
submoustachial stripe

median crown stripe
lateral crown stripe
supraloral area
lore
malar stripe

Lark Sparrow

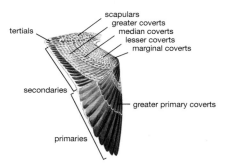

tertials

scapulars
greater coverts
median coverts
lesser coverts
marginal coverts

secondaries

greater primary coverts

primaries

Great Black-backed Gull, upper wing

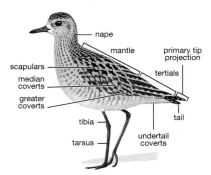

nape
mantle
primary tip projection
tertials
scapulars
median coverts
greater coverts
tibia
tarsus
undertail coverts
tail

Pacific Golden-Plover

An entry begins with **Field Marks**, the physical clues used to quickly identify a bird, such as body shape and size, bill length, and plumage color or pattern. A bird's body parts yield vital clues to identification, so a birder needs to become familiar with them early on. After the first glance at body type, take note of the head shape and markings, such as stripes, eye rings, and crown markings. Bill shape and color are important as well. Note body and wing details: wing bars, color of and pattern of wing feathers at rest, and shape and markings when extended in flight. Tail shape, length, color, and banding may play a big part, too. At left are diagrams detailing the various parts of a bird—its topography—labeled with the term likely to be found in the text of this book.

The main body of each entry is divided into three categories: Behavior, Habitat, and Local Sites. The **Behavior** section details certain characteristics to look or listen for in the field. Often a bird's behavioral characteristics are very closely related to its body type and field marks, such as in the case of woodpeckers, whose stiff tails, strong legs, and sharp claws enable them to spend most of their lives in an upright position, braced against a tree trunk. The **Habitat** section describes areas that are most likely to support the featured species. Preferred nesting locations of breeding birds are also included in many cases. The **Local Sites** section recommends specific refuges or parks where the featured bird is likely to be found. A section called **Field Notes** finishes each entry, and includes information such as plumage variations within a species; or it may introduce another species with which the featured bird is frequently confused. In either case, an additional drawing may be included to aid in identification.

Finally, a caption under each of the photographs gives the season of the plumage pictured, as well as the age and sex of the bird, if discernable. A key to using this informative guide and its range maps follows on the next two pages.

READING THE SPREAD

1 Photograph: Shows bird in habitat. May be female or male, adult or juvenile. Plumage may be breeding, molting, nonbreeding, or year-round.

2 Caption: Defines the featured bird's plumage, age, and sometimes sex, as seen in the picture.

3 Heading: Beneath the common name find the Latin, or scientific, name. Beside it is the bird's length (L), and sometimes its wingspan (WS). Wingspan is given with birds often seen in flight. Female measurements are given if noticeably different from male.

4 Field Marks: Gives basic facts for field identification: markings, head and bill shape, and body size.

5 Band: Gives the common name of the bird's family.

6 Range Map: Shows year-round range in purple, breeding range in

red, winter range in blue. Areas through which species are likely to migrate are shown in green.

7 Behavior: A step beyond **Field Marks**, gives clues to identifying a bird by its habits, such as feeding, flight pattern, courtship, nest-building, or songs and calls.

8 Habitat: Reveals the area a species is most likely to inhabit, such as forests, marshes, grasslands, or urban areas. May include preferred nesting sites.

9 Local Sites: Details local spots to look for the given species.

10 Field Notes: A special entry that may give a unique point of identification, compare two species of the same family, compare two species from different families that are easily confused, or focus on a historical or conservation fact.

On each map of Pennsylvania, range boundaries are drawn beyond which the species is not regularly seen. Nearly every species will be rare at the edges of its range. The sample map shown below explains the colors and symbols used on each map. Ranges continually expand and contract, so the map is a tool, not a rule. Range information is based on actual sightings and therefore depends upon the number of knowledgeable and active birders in each area.

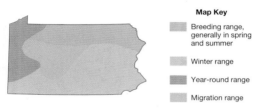

Map Key

Breeding range, generally in spring and summer

Winter range

Year-round range

Migration range

Sample Map: Hooded Merganser

READING THE INDEXES

There are two indexes at the back of this book. The first is a **Color Index** (p. 262), created to help birders quickly find an entry by noting its color in the field. In this index, male birds are labeled by their predominant color: Mostly White, Mostly Black, etc. Note that a bird may have a head of a different color than its label states. That's because its body—the part most noticeable in the field—is the color labeled.

The **Alphabetical Index** (p. 266) is organized by the bird's common name. Next to each entry is a check-off box. Most birders make lists of the birds they see. Some keep several lists, perhaps one of birds in a certain area and another of all the birds they've ever seen—a life list. Such lists enable birders to look back and remember their first sighting of an Indigo Bunting or an American Kestrel.

Year-round | Adult white morph

SNOW GOOSE

Chen caerulescens L 31" (79 cm) WS 56" (142 cm)

FIELD MARKS

White overall

Black primaries show in flight

Heavy pinkish bill with black "grinning patch"

Juvenile is dingy gray-brown on head, neck, and upperparts

Behavior

Travels in large flocks, especially during spring migration. Loud, vocal birds that sound like baying hounds, flocks migrate in loose V-formation and long lines, sometimes more than 1,500 miles nonstop, reaching speeds up to 40 mph. Primarily vegetarian, forages on agricultural grains and plants and aquatic vegetation. An agile swimmer, commonly rests on water during migration and at wintering grounds. Listen for its harsh, descending *whouk,* heard continuously in flight.

Habitat

Most often seen on grasslands, grainfields, and wetlands, favoring standing shallow freshwater marshes and flooded fields. Breeds in the Arctic.

Local Sites

Middle Creek Wildlife Management Area offers the state's greatest spectacle, where as many as 200,000 migrants may stop to rest and refuel in late February and early March.

FIELD NOTES Amid a flock of white Snow Geese, you may see a few dark morphs as well, characterized by a varying amount of dark gray-brown on the back and breast (inset). These birds were formerly considered a separate species, the Blue Goose.

Year-round | Adult

CANADA GOOSE

Branta canadensis L 30-43" (75-108 cm) WS 59-73" (148-183 cm)

FIELD MARKS

Black head and neck marked with distinctive white chin strap

In flight, shows large, dark wings, white undertail coverts, and a long protruding neck

Brown body, paler below; white vent and belly

Behavior

A common, familiar goose; best known for migrating in large V-formation. Like some other members of its family, finds a mate and remains monogamous for life. Nests on the ground in open or forested areas near water. Its distinctive honking call makes it easy to identify, even without seeing it. Males give a lower-pitched *hwonk*, females a higher *hrink*.

Habitat

Prefers wetlands, grasslands, and cultivated fields within commuting distance of water. Has also adapted successfully to man-made habitats such as golf courses, landscaped ponds, and farms.

Local Sites

Virtually every lake and pond in Pennsylvania hosts year-round residents. Thousands of migrants and winterers are regular visitors in the Pymatuning area and Middle Creek Wildlife Management Area.

FIELD NOTES Research into the mitochondrial DNA of the Canada Goose has found that the smaller sub-species, such as *hutchinsii* (inset, left) and *minima* (inset, right), actually belong to their own species, the newly named Cackling Goose, *Branta hutchinsii*.

Year-round | Adults

TUNDRA SWAN

Cygnus columbianus L 52" (132 cm)

FIELD MARKS

White overall

Black, slightly concave bill with yellow spot of variable size in front of eye

Juvenile appears darker with pinkish bill

Behavior

Feeds on aquatic vegetation in shallow water, utilizing its long neck, which enables it to keep its body upright. Flies in straight lines or in V-formation, with its neck protruding forward. Utilizing the same routes every year, the Tundra Swan migrates thousands of miles between Arctic breeding grounds and temperate wintering quarters. Call is a noisy, barking *kwooo*, often heard at night.

Habitat

Winters in coastal areas on ponds, lakes, estuaries, and marshes. Breeds on ponds in Alaska and the Arctic.

Local Sites

These swans' main migration route passes through Pennsylvania, and large numbers stop to rest and feed at Middle Creek Wildlife Management Area, on the lower Susquehanna River, and at large lakes in Moraine and Yellow Creek State Parks.

FIELD NOTES The introduced Mute Swan, *Cygnus olor* (inset: juvenile, left; adult, right), has a black knob at the base of an orange bill. At rest, the Mute Swan holds its neck in an S-curve, bill pointed down; the Tundra Swan's neck is straight. Mute Swans are rare year-round residents in Pennsylvania.

Breeding | Adult male

WOOD DUCK

Aix sponsa L 18.5" (47 cm)

FIELD MARKS
Male has glossy iridescent head and crest, lined in white; red, white, black, and yellow bill; burgundy breast with white spotting; yellowish sides

Female duller overall with large white teardrop-shaped eye patch

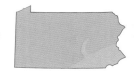

Behavior
Most commonly feeds by picking insects from the water's surface or by tipping into shallows to pluck invertebrates from the bottom, but may also be seen foraging on land. The omnivorous Wood Duck's diet changes throughout the year depending upon available foods and its need for particular proteins or minerals during migration, breeding, and molting. Nests in tree cavities or man-made nest boxes. Male Wood Ducks give a soft, upslurred whistle when swimming. Female Wood Ducks have a distinctive rising, squealing flight call of *ooEEK*.

Habitat
Inhabits woodlands and forested swamps.

Local Sites
This species can be found at almost any woodland-fringed wetland. Large numbers congregate after breeding at Pymatuning State Park, Erie National Wildlife Refuge, Moraine State Park, and on the Delaware River.

FIELD NOTES The Wood Duck female (inset) hatches up to 15 eggs in cavities high up in trees or nest boxes. Once hatched, the young must make a long jump to the water, sometimes 30 feet below. Protected by their downy plumage, they generally land safely.

Year-round | Male

AMERICAN BLACK DUCK

Anas rubripes L 23" (58 cm)

FIELD MARKS
Blackish brown body, paler on
face and foreneck

In flight, white wing linings
contrast sharply with dark body;
violet speculum bordered in black

Male's bill is yellow, female's is
dull green

Behavior
Feeds in shallow water, mostly on aquatic vegetation in
winter and aquatic insects in summer. Female builds
nest of plant material and downy feathers in a shallow
depression on the ground. The female Black Duck gives
a typical loud *QUACK*; the male's call is shorter and
lower-pitched.

Habitat
Found in woodland lakes and streams and in coastal
marshes, often in the company of Mallards.

Local Sites
These birds nest sparingly throughout the state, but are
most often seen in migrating and wintering flocks on
the Delaware and lower Susquehanna rivers, at
Pymatuning State Park, and in the Middle Creek
Wildlife Management Area.

FIELD NOTES The population of the American Black Duck seems
to be losing ground due to increased deforestation and displacement by the highly adaptable Mallard, with which the Black Duck
often hybridizes. The breeding male Mal-
lard is easily set apart by his green hood
and grayish body, but the female Mallard
(inset) more closely resembles the Black
Duck. Look for her warmer brown body,
orange bill with dark center, and blue
speculum bordered in white.

Breeding | Adult male

MALLARD

Anas platyrhynchos L 23" (58 cm)

FIELD MARKS

Male has metallic green head and neck; white collar; chestnut breast

Female mottled brown overall; orange bill marked with black

Both sexes have bright blue speculum bordered in white; white tail and underwings

Behavior

A dabbler, the Mallard feeds by "tipping up" in shallow water and plucking seeds, grasses, and invertebrates from the bottom. Also picks insects from the water's surface. The courtship ritual of the Mallard consists of the male pumping his head, dipping his bill, and rearing up in the water to exaggerate his size. A female signals consent by duplicating the male's head-pumping. Nests on the ground in concealing vegetation. The Mallard female is known for her loud, descending *QUACK*. The male's call is shorter, softer, less commonly given.

Habitat

This widespread species occurs wherever shallow fresh water is found, from rural swamps to city ponds.

Local Sites

Look for Mallards at almost any lake, pond, river, or other wetland.

FIELD NOTES At first glance, the bright green head of the male Northern Shoveler, *Anas clypeata* (inset: female, left; male, right), can be mistaken for the Mallard's. Look for the Shoveler's large, dark, spatulate bill—a telltale mark on both sexes. The Northern Shoveler winters regularly in southeastern Pennsylvania.

Breeding | Adult male

NORTHERN PINTAIL

Anas acuta Male L 26" (66 cm) Female L 20" (51 cm)

FIELD MARKS

Male has chocolate brown head; long white neck stripes, breast, and underparts; gray back; long black central tail feathers

Female mottled brown overall

Long neck, slender body, and pointed tail evident in flight

Behavior

Often seen in small flocks during winter months, foraging for seeds in flooded agricultural fields or shallow ponds and marshes. Also eats aquatic insects, snails, beetles, and small crustaceans. This elegant duck is an accomplished flyer known for spilling out of the sky in spectacular rapid descents and leveling out directly into a landing. Male's call while breeding is a high, whining *mee-meee;* female utters a weak *quack.*

Habitat

Frequents both freshwater and saltwater marshes, ponds, lakes, and bays. Also found in flooded agricultural fields, especially during winter.

Local Sites

The best places to see migratory pintails are Pymatuning State Park, Geneva Marsh, Lake Ontelaunee, and other large lakes. In winter, look for them at John Heinz National Wildlife Refuge.

FIELD NOTES The Northern Pintail female engages in an elaborate in-flight courtship ritual in which she veers, swerves, makes abrupt turns, and climbs, challenging her suitor to match her moves. If he succeeds, she rewards the male by allowing him to take her tail in his beak, or to pass below her so closely that their wing tips touch. If he fails her test, the female signals to another male to make an attempt.

Breeding | Adult male

GREEN-WINGED TEAL

Anas crecca L 14.5" (37 cm)

FIELD MARKS

Male's chestnut head has green ear patch

Female has mottled, dusky brown upperparts; white belly and undertail coverts

In flight, shows green speculum bordered above in buff

Behavior

Like other dabbling ducks, the Green-winged teal feeds at the water's surface or upended, tail in the air and head submerged, to reach aquatic plants, seeds, and invertebrates. An agile and fast-moving flier, it travels in small flocks that twist and turn erratically in midair. The Green-winged Teal migrates late, peaking in mid- to late October, and winters very far north–as far as Newfoundland–for such a small and cold-vulnerable duck. Nests are hidden among grasses and weeds, within 200 feet of water. The Green-winged female emits a high, thin *quack*; the male gives a sharp,whistled *kreek*.

Habitat

Found on shallow lakes and inland ponds, especially those with standing or floating vegetation. Also forages on mudflats.

Local Sites

Look for migrants at Pymatuning, Moraine, and Yellow Creek State Parks. Many spend the winter at John Heinz National Wildlife Refuge.

FIELD NOTES The bill of the Green-winged Teal is specialized for filtering food from mud. The edges of both of its mandibles are lined with tiny, comb-like structures called lamellae. These structures allow the birds to strain even microscopic food matter from the bottoms of lakes and ponds.

Breeding | Adult male

CANVASBACK

Aythya valisineria L 21" (53 cm)

FIELD MARKS

Male's head and neck are chestnut; back and sides whitish; breast and tail black

Female's head, neck, and breast are pale brown; back and sides pale gray

Forehead slopes to long, black bill

Behavior

Feeds on the water in large flocks, diving deep for fish, mollusks, and vegetation. Its heavy body requires a running start on water for takeoff. Flocks fly fairly high in lines or in irregular V-formation. Walks awkwardly, but not often seen on land. Both sexes are generally silent.

Habitat

Found in marshes, on lakes, and along large rivers. Breeds in thick marsh grasses on upper Great Plains and north through Canada to Alaska, where it is a frequent victim of brood parasitism by the closely related Redhead.

Local Sites

Migrants stop, at least briefly, at all large lakes. In winter, thousands of birds may remain at Presque Isle State Park and smaller numbers congregate on the Delaware River.

FIELD NOTES Sharing the male Canvasback's rufous head and neck, the male Redhead, *Aythya americana* (inset), can be difficult to distinguish in the field. Look for its grayer back, its tricolored bill of pale blue, white, and black, and for its yellow eyes—the Canvasback's eyes are red. The two species share much of the same range and nesting locations.

Breeding | Adult male

RING-NECKED DUCK

Aythya collaris L 17" (43 cm)

FIELD MARKS
Male has glossy purple head, breast, back, and tail; pale gray sides

Female is brown with pale face patch, eye ring, and eye stripe

Peaked crown; blue-gray bill with white ring and black tip

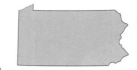

Behavior
An expert diver, the Ring-necked can feed on aquatic plants as deep as 40 feet below the water's surface, but tends to remain in shallower waters. Small flocks can be seen diving in shallow water for plants, roots, and seeds. Unlike most other diving ducks, the Ring-necked springs into flight directly from water, and flies in loose flocks with rapid wing beats. Though often silent, the female sometimes gives a harsh, grating *deeer*.

Habitat
Fairly common in freshwater marshes and on woodland ponds and small lakes. Also found in marshes along large rivers in winter. Breeds across boreal forests of Canada and into the northern United States.

Local Sites
Presque Isle, Moraine, and Yellow Creek State Parks are good spots to find migrants. Large numbers of Ring-necked Ducks may remain into the winter at Presque Isle State Park, and many spend all winter on the lower Delaware River.

FIELD NOTES The distinctive field mark that gives this duck its name is actually quite hard to spot in the field. At close range and with the right amount of light, you may be able to spot the male's fine ring of brownish iridescence (pictured opposite) that separates his glossy purple head from his black breast.

Breeding | Adult male

LESSER SCAUP

Aythya affinis L 16.5" (42 cm)

FIELD MARKS
Black head is slightly peaked,
sometimes with purplish gloss

Black neck and breast, black tail;
black-and-white barred back;
white sides

Female has brown head, neck,
upperparts; white at base of bill

Behavior
One of North America's most abundant diving ducks
perhaps due to its omnivorous diet. Forages for aquatic
insects, mollusks, snails, leeches, crustaceans, and small
fish. Dives to sift through mud for seeds and aquatic
vegetation. Both sexes are generally silent.

Habitat
Large flocks can be found in winter in sheltered bays,
inlets, lakes, and rivers. Some birds may also wander
farther afield to agricultural fields and marshes.

Local Sites
Flocks sometimes spend the winter at Presque Isle State
Park, on the lower Susquehanna River, and at John
Heinz National Wildlife Refuge. Migrants appear in
good numbers at virtually all large lakes across
the state.

FIELD NOTES The Greater
Scaup, *Aythya marila* (inset:
male, left; female, right), very
closely resembles the Lesser in both sexes. The Greater's more
rounded head is its most distinguishable field mark. The larger
amount of white on the Greater Scaup's wings is another helpful
field mark. The Greater Scaup generally keeps to the Lake Erie
shore during migration and winter, while the Lesser is more likely
to be found inland on freshwater lakes and ponds.

Breeding | Adult male

BUFFLEHEAD

Bucephala albeola   L 13.5" (34 cm)

FIELD MARKS
Small duck with large puffy head, steep forehead, and short bill

Male has large white head patch and a glossy black back

Female is gray-brown overall with small, elongated white patches on either side of her head

Behavior
Often seen in small flocks, some birds keeping a lookout while others dive for aquatic insects, snails, and small fish. Like all diving ducks, its feet are set well back on its body to swiftly propel it through the water. Able to take off directly out of water, unlike many other diving ducks. Monogamous, Buffleheads are believed to stay with the same mate for years and to faithfully return to the same nesting site each season. Both sexes are generally silent away from the breeding grounds.

Habitat
Found on sheltered bays, rivers, and lakes in winter. Breeds primarily in Canada.

Local Sites
Presque Isle and Moraine State Parks, John Heinz National Wildlife Refuge, and Lake Ontelaunee are prime locations to see large numbers of these birds in migration and winter.

FIELD NOTES In its boreal forest breeding grounds in Canada, this smallest of North American diving ducks nests almost exclusively in cavities created by the Northern Flicker (*Colaptes auratus*); a nesting site so tiny that it is speculated to have influenced the Bufflehead's own small size.

Breeding | Adult male

COMMON GOLDENEYE

Bucephala clangula L 18.5" (47 cm)

FIELD MARKS

Head black with greenish tinge on breeding male, brown on female

Male has white patches between eyes and bill; female has white neck ring and gray breast

Male is black above with white scapulars; female grayish above

Behavior

A diving duck, may be seen foraging in flocks, often with much of the flock diving simultaneously for aqautic insects, invertebrates, and plants. With feet located near its tail, this bird is an expert swimmer and diver, but walks very awkwardly on land. Male is generally silent outside of breeding grounds, but female occasionally gives a harsh, croaking *gack*. Listen as well for the low, stirring whistle made by the wings of the adult male in flight.

Habitat

Inhabits deep, open lakes and rivers near woodlands. In winter, also found in coastal areas. Look for this hardy duck even in open water between ice floes.

Local Sites

These birds are best seen in migration and during winter months at Presque Isle and Pymatuning State Parks, the lower Susquehanna River, and John Heinz National Wildlife Refuge.

FIELD NOTES Distinctive marks to look for in the field on the female Common Goldeneye (inset) include her brown head, yellowish eye, mostly black bill with a yellowish tip, and her white neck ring. Both sexes show a large amount of white on their wings in flight.

Breeding | Adult male

HOODED MERGANSER

Lophodytes cucullatus L 18" (46 cm)

FIELD MARKS
Puffy, rounded crest

Male's white head patches are fan-shaped and conspicuous; black bill, back, and tail; white breast with two vertical black bars; chestnut sides

Female brownish gray overall with a rusty brown crest

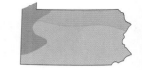

Behavior
Dives expertly, using its wings and feet to propel itself underwater. Serrated bill is good for catching fish; also feeds on crustaceans, insects, and plants. Known at times to hunt cooperatively with other merganser species. Takes flight directly out of water, and moves swiftly with rapid wing beats. Though generally silent, throaty grunts and chatter can sometimes be heard from these ducks. A displaying drake will also emit a froglike growl.

Habitat
Winters on fresh and brackish water. In breeding season, found on woodland ponds, rivers, and backwaters, especially swamps.

Local Sites
In the breeding season look for these birds in wooded wetlands, especially Pymatuning State Park and Erie National Wildlife Refuge; during migration at Pymatuning, Presque Isle, and Moraine State Parks; in winter on the lower Susquehanna and Delaware Rivers.

FIELD NOTES A distinctive field mark on the female Hooded Merganser (inset) is her thin, serrated bill with a dark upper mandible and a yellowish lower one. In flight, note both sexes' crests are flattened.

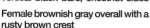

Breeding | Adult male, left; adult female, right

COMMON MERGANSER

Mergus merganser L 25" (64 cm)

FIELD MARKS
Breeding male has blackish green
head and black back

Female and nonbreeding male have
chestnut head and gray back

Long, slim neck

Thin, hooked red bill

Behavior
Swiftly gives chase to small fish, which it catches with
its long, thin, serrated bill. Also eats mollusks, crustaceans, and aquatic insects. Flies low with rapid wing
beats, following the courses of rivers and streams. Joins
single-sex flocks of 10 to 20 birds, until late winter
when pairs form. Nests in tree cavities and rock
crevices near lakes and rivers. Though generally silent,
harsh croaks can be heard from the male during
courtship and when alarmed.

Habitat
Prefers the still, open water of large lakes, but may also
be found in rivers of wooded areas, especially in winter.

Local Sites
Common Mergansers breed in Allegheny National Forest and Delaware Water Gap National Recreation Area.
In migration and winter, they are especially common
on the lower Delaware and Susquehanna Rivers.

FIELD NOTES The Red-breasted Merganser, *Mergus serrator* (inset:
female), is a common migrant through Pennsylvania. The female
has a brown head, less distinctly outlined than the Common's; the
male has a green head, a white collar, a
streaked brown breast, and gray
flanks. Note the shaggy double
crest on both sexes.

Year-round | Adult male

RING-NECKED PHEASANT

Phasianus colchicus Male L 33" (84 cm) Female L 21" (53 cm)

FIELD MARKS
Male iridescent bronze, mottled
with black, brown, and gray

Female buffy overall with dark
spotting and barring

Male has fleshy red face patches

Long tail; short, rounded wings

Behavior
This introduced Eurasian species feeds primarily on
seeds and grain, but will also eat weeds, buds, berries,
and insects. Like other game birds, the Ring-necked has
a crop in which it stores food, reducing the amount of
time required for it to forage in the open. Tends to run
rather than fly, but if flushed, this bird rises almost vertically with a loud whirring of its wings. Nests on the
ground in a shallow depression made by the female.
Male's territorial call is a loud, penetrating *kok-cack*.
Both sexes give hoarse, croaking alarm notes.

Habitat
Inhabits open country, farmlands, brushy areas, and
woodland edges.

Local Sites
This species is declining severely, but look for it year-
round on state game lands or in farmland areas.

FIELD NOTES The Ring-necked Pheasant has been continually
reintroduced into different regions of North America since the
mid-1800s for purposes of hunting. First introduced into Pennsylvania in 1915, populations of Ring-neckeds have been difficult
to maintain during the last 20 years due to harsh winters of
heavy snowfall and new farming methods. More than 200,000
birds are brought to Pennsylvania annually from China and England, producing subspecies hybrids of variable plumage.

Year-round | Adult gray morph

RUFFED GROUSE

Bonasa umbellus L 17" (43 cm)

FIELD MARKS

Grayish or redddish brown overall, mottled with white

Small crest; multibanded tail

Black ruff on neck, usually inconspicuous

Wide, dark band near tip of tail

Behavior

Forages on the ground primarily for seeds, nuts, fruit, and berries. Its diet varies by season, and may also include insects, amphibians, and small reptiles. If flushed, bursts into flight with a roar of its wings. Emits nasal squeals and clucks, especially when alarmed.

Habitat

A woodland bird which tends to remain in deciduous or mixed forests with brushy cover. May also be found near forest clearings.

Local Sites

Pennsylvania's official state bird has become uncommon and hard to find in most areas; look for it in any large forest or small woodland throughout the year. The reddish morph is the most widespread form in Pennsylvania.

FIELD NOTES The Ruffed Grouse is generally shy, elusive, and found singly, except in spring when the male (inset: gray morph) claims his territory and attracts females by raising his crest and neck ruff, fanning his tail and beating his wings rapidly, making a hollow, accelerating, drumming noise as he struts. This low-frequency noise is often said to be felt as much as heard.

Year-round | Adult male

WILD TURKEY

Meleagris gallopavo Male L 46" (117 cm) Female L 37" (94 cm)

FIELD MARKS

Large, with purple, green,and bronze iridescent plumage

Unfeathered blue and pink head with red wattles

Male has blackish breast tuft

Female smaller, less iridescent

Behavior

Largest of game birds, the turkey lives communally in small flocks. A ground feeder by day, the Wild Turkey roosts in trees at night. Forages for nuts, seeds, fruit, insects, frogs, and lizards. Flies well for short distances when alarmed, but prefers to walk or run. Females raise large broods, nesting in leaf-lined hollows in brush or woodlands. Male's characteristic display during breeding season involves puffing out his chest, swelling his wattles, spreading his tail, and rattling his wings, all while gobbling and strutting. In spring, the male's gobbling call may be heard from as far as a mile away.

Habitat

Frequents open forests, grainfields and forest edges.

Local Sites

Increasing numbers of turkeys are present in the Allegheny National Forest, the Delaware Water Gap National Recreation Area, and woodlands of any size— even amid developed areas.

FIELD NOTES At the First Continental Congress held in Philadelphia in 1774, Benjamin Franklin argued for the turkey to be named the national bird, stating "He is besides, though a little vain & silly, a Bird of Courage, and would not hesitate to attack a Grenadier of the British Guards who should presume to invade his Farm Yard with a Red Coat on."

Nonbreeding | Adult

COMMON LOON

Gavia immer L 32" (81 cm)

FIELD MARKS
In winter: dark gray above, pale below; blue-gray bill; dark nape has white indentation each side

In spring and summer: back black-and-white checked; head dark green; neck striped; black bill

Behavior
A diving bird; eats fish up to 10 inches long, which it grasps with its pointed beak. Forages by diving and swimming underwater, propelled by large, paddle-shaped feet. Can stay submerged for up to three minutes at depths down to 250 feet. It is nearly impossible for the Common Loon to walk on land. Generally remains silent on wintering grounds.

Habitat
Winters in coastal waters, or inland on large lakes.

Local Sites
Presque Isle, Pymatuning, and Yellow Creek State Parks, and Lake Ontelaunee are prime locations to find these birds during spring and fall migrations. Hundreds of fall migrants may pass over Hawk Mountain Sanctuary and Waggoner's Gap in a single day.

FIELD NOTES The eponymous dark red throat patch of the Red-throated Loon, *Gavia stellata* (inset: nonbreeding), is visible only during breeding season. In winter, the Red-throated can be identified by the sharply defined white on its face, which extends farther back than that on the Common Loon, and by its habit of holding its thinner bill angled slightly upward.

Breeding | Adult

PIED-BILLED GREBE

Podilymbus podiceps L 13.5" (34 cm)

FIELD MARKS
Small and short-necked

Breeding adult brownish gray overall; black ring around stout, whitish bill; black chin and throat

Winter birds lose bill ring; chin becomes white; plumage is browner overall

Behavior
The most widespread of North American grebes, the Pied-billed remains for the most part on water, seldom on land or in flight. Dives for aquatic insects, small fish, frogs, and vegetable matter. When alarmed, it slowly sinks, holding only its head above the water's surface. Like most grebes, the Pied-billed eats its own feathers and feeds them to its young, perhaps to protect their stomach linings from fish bones or animal shells. Song is a series of slightly hollow, rapid-paced *kuh-kuh-kuh*s or *k'owh-k'owh-k'owh*s.

Habitat
Prefers nesting around freshwater marshes and ponds. Also found in more open waters of large bays and rivers. Winters on both fresh and salt water.

Local Sites
Look for breeding birds in the Pymatuning region, Erie National Wildlife Refuge, and Allegheny National Forest. Migrants stop at most lakes in both spring and fall.

FIELD NOTES The stark black-and-white Horned Grebe, *Podiceps auritus* (inset: non-breeding), is a common spring and fall migrant throughout Pennsylvania; it is also found in winter in the southeastern portion of the state.

Immature

DOUBLE-CRESTED CORMORANT

Phalacrocorax auritus L 32" (81 cm) W 52" (132 cm)

FIELD MARKS

Black overall; facial skin yellow-orange; pale bill hooked at tip

Distinctive kinked neck in flight

Breeding adult has tufts of black feathers behind eyes

Immature has pale neck and breast

Behavior

In pursuit of prey, the Double-crested can dive to considerable depths, propelling itself with fully webbed feet. Uses its hooked bill to grasp fish. Feeds on a variety of aquatic life. May swim submerged to the neck, bill pointed slightly skyward. When it leaves the water, it perches on a branch, dock, or piling and half-spreads its wings to dry (pictured opposite). Soars at times, its neck in an S-shape. Nests near water either in trees or on rocks. Silent for the most part, but sometimes emits a deep grunt.

Habitat

Found along coasts, at inland lakes, and near rivers; it has adapted to fresh and saltwater environments.

Local Sites

The Delaware, Allegheny, and Susquehanna Rivers are major migration routes for these birds in both spring and fall.

FIELD NOTES The immature Double-crested (inset: first year) shows a large amount of white and pale gray on its neck and breast. Its back and wings are a dark gray-brown with pale edging to the feathers and its bill is extensively yellow or pale orange. This coloration is not lost completely until the third year, though older immatures may resemble nonbreeding adults.

Breeding | Adult

GREAT BLUE HERON

Ardea herodias L 46" (117 cm) WS 72" (183 cm)

FIELD MARKS

Gray-blue overall; white foreneck with black streaks; yellowish bill

Black stripe extends above eye

Breeding adult has plumes on its head, neck, and back

Juvenile has dark crown; no plumes

Behavior

Waits for prey to come into its range, then spears it with a quick thrust of its sharp bill. Eats almost anything, from fish, snakes, and frogs, to mice and woodchucks, to large insects and some small birds. Flies with its head folded back onto its shoulders in an S-curve, typical of other herons as well. When threatened, draws its neck back with plumes erect and points its bill at antagonist. Pairs build stick nests high in trees in loose association with other Great Blue pairs. Mostly silent away from its nest, but sometimes emits an annoyed, deep, guttural *kraaank* as it takes flight.

Habitat

Hunts for aquatic creatures in marshes and swamps, and for small mammals in fields and forest edges.

Local Sites

These birds dwell at lakes, ponds, marshy wetlands, and rivers year-round wherever waters remain ice free.

FIELD NOTES The adult Black-crowned Night-Heron, *Nycticorax nycticorax* (inset), at 25" tall, is smaller than the Great Blue with a black crown and back, gray upperwings and rump, and white underparts. Primarily nocturnal, the Black-crowned is hard to find outside of its breeding colonies at John Heinz National Wildlife Refuge, along the Susquehanna River, and at Pymatuning Swamp.

Breeding | Adult

GREAT EGRET

Ardea alba L 39" (99 cm) WS 51" (130 cm)

FIELD MARKS

Large white heron with heavy yellow bill, black legs and feet

Breeding adult has long plumes trailing from its back, extending beyond the tail

Blue-green lores while breeding

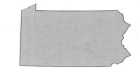

Behavior

Stalks its prey slowly and methodically in shallow water, uses its sharply pointed bill to capture small fish, aquatic insects, frogs, and crayfish. Also known to hunt snakes, birds, and small mammals. Occasionally forages in groups or steals food from smaller birds. The Great Egret makes its nest in trees or shrubs 10 to 40 feet above the ground. Colonies may have as many as a hundred birds. Generally silent except when nesting or disturbed, when it may emit a guttural *kraak* or repeated *cuk-cuk-cuk* notes.

Habitat

Inhabits both freshwater and saltwater wetlands.

Local Sites

Look for breeding individuals or small groups on the lower Susquehanna and Delaware Rivers and for non-breeding wanderers at Moraine, Yellow Creek, and Marsh Creek State Parks from late spring to early fall.

FIELD NOTES Early in the breeding season, the Great Egret grows long, ostentatious feathers called aigrettes from its scapulars. In the late 1800s, aigrettes were so sought after by the millinery industry that Great Egrets were hunted nearly to extinction. The grassroots campaign to end the slaughter later developed into the National Audubon Society. Today, loss of wetlands continues to limit the population of Great Egrets and other herons.

Year-round | Adult

GREEN HERON

Butorides virescens L 18" (46 cm) WS 26" (66 cm)

FIELD MARKS

Small, chunky heron with blue-green back and crown, sometimes raised to form shaggy crest

Back and sides of neck deep chestnut, throat white

Short yellow to orange legs

Behavior

Usually a solitary hunter, a Green Heron that lands near one of its kind is likely to be attacked. Stands motionless in or near water, waiting for a fish to come close enough for a swift attack. Spends most of its day in the shade, sometimes perched in trees or shrubs. When alarmed, it may make a show by flicking its tail, raising its crest, and elongating its neck. Both sexes build nest in tree or shrub, generally not far from the ground. A sharp *skeow* may be heard in flight.

Habitat

Found in a variety of wetland habitats but prefers streams, ponds, and marshes with woodland cover.

Local Sites

Breeders and migrants are widespread at wooded lakes, marshes, and other wetlands. Presque Isle State Park, Lake Ontelaunee, and Lake Nockamixon are all good places to seek these birds.

FIELD NOTES An innovative hunter, the Green Heron will sometimes, though rarely, stand at the edge of shallow water and toss twigs, insects, even earthworms into the water as lures to attract unsuspecting minnows into its striking range. This is one of the few instances of tool use in the bird world.

Year-round | Adult

TURKEY VULTURE

Cathartes aura L 27" (69 cm) WS 69" (175 cm)

FIELD MARKS

In flight, contrasting two-toned underwings; long tail extends beyond feet

Brownish black feathers on body; silver gray flight feathers

Unfeathered red head; ivory bill; head and bill black on juvenile

Behavior

An adept flier, the Turkey Vulture soars high above the ground in search of carrion and refuse. Rocks from side to side in flight, seldom flapping its wings. Well developed sense of smell allows the Turkey Vulture to locate carrion concealed in forest settings. Feeds heavily when food is available but can go days without if necessary. Nests solitarily in abandoned buildings or hollow logs and trees. Generally silent, but will emit soft hisses and grunts while feeding or if threatened.

Habitat

Hunts in open country and woodlands, and in urban dumps and landfills. Often seen over highways.

Local Sites

Though these birds are conspicuous everywhere, they are known to gather in spectacular numbers at Gettysburg National Military Park, where over 1,000 have been counted.

FIELD NOTES The less common Black Vulture, *Coragyps atratus* (inset), is not as efficient at finding a meal, but is more aggressive. It will sometimes follow a Turkey Vulture to its find and claim it as its own. Look for the Black Vulture's shorter tail and white restricted to the primaries.

Year-round | Adult

OSPREY

Pandion haliaetus L 22-25" (56-64 cm) WS 58-72" (147-183 cm)

FIELD MARKS

Dark brown above, white below; white head, dark eye stripe; females usually have darker neck streaks

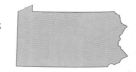

Slightly arched in flight, wings appear bent back or "crooked"

Pale plumage fringing in juvenile

Behavior

Hunts by soaring, hovering, then diving down and plunging feet-first into water, snatching its prey with long, lethal talons. Feeds exclusively on fish. The Osprey's specialized diet makes it susceptible to accumulating contaminants, such as DDT. Nests near bodies of fresh or salt water. Bulky nests are built atop dead trees or on specialized man-made platforms. Call is a series of clear, resonant, whistled *kyew*s.

Habitat

Forages in a variety of aquatic habitats, including lakes, rivers, and reservoirs. Highly migratory, these birds can be found on every continent except Antarctica.

Local Sites

Nesters are conspicuous at Shenango Reservoir, Moraine State Park, the lower Susquehanna, and lakes in the Pocono Mountains. Fall migrants are seen daily at Hawk Mountain Sanctuary on Kittatinny Ridge.

FIELD NOTES The use of DDT and other chemical pollutants during the 1950s and 1960s decimated the Osprey population in Pennsylvania; by 1979, no Ospreys could be found in the state. Since then, reintroduction programs have made them once again regular breeders around Pennsylvannia's lakes and rivers.

Year-round | Adult

BALD EAGLE

Haliaeetus leucocephalus L 31-37" (79-94 cm) WS 70-90" (178-229 cm)

FIELD MARKS
Distinctive white head and tail

Large yellow beak, feet, and eyes

Brown body

Juveniles mostly dark, showing blotchy white on underwing and tail

Behavior
The national bird of the United States. A rock-steady flier, the Bald Eagle rarely swerves or tips on its flattened wings. Feeds mainly on fish, but sometimes on waterfowl, carrion, or small mammals. Often steals fish from other birds of prey. Bald Eagles lock talons and cartwheel together through the sky in an elaborate courtship dance. Nests solitarily in tall trees or on cliffs. Call is a weak, almost inaudible *kak-kak-kak.*

Habitat
This member of the sea-eagle group generally lives and feeds along seacoasts or along rivers and lakes.

Local Sites
Among more than 100 nesting pairs in the state, those at Pymatuning State Park are easiest to see. Migrants are frequent along the Kittatinny Ridge, the lower Susquehanna River, and the Delaware River.

FIELD NOTES An immature Bald Eagle (inset: second year) shows a variable amount of white spotting on its head, breast, and underwings. It is not until its fifth year that it acquires the characteristic stark white head of the adult.

Year-round | Adult male

NORTHERN HARRIER

Circus cyaneus L 17-23" (43-58 cm) WS 38-48" (97-122 cm)

FIELD MARKS

Adult male grayish above, white below; female brown, white below with brown streaks

Slim body; long, narrow wings

Long tail with white on the rump

Juvenile cinnamon brown below

Behavior

Generally perches low and flies close to the ground, wings upraised, searching for birds, mice, frogs, and other prey. Seldom soars high except during migration and in an exuberant, acrobatic courtship display, when the male loops and somersaults in the air. Often found hunting in the dim light of dawn or dusk. During winter, roosts communally on the ground. Nests on the ground. Identifiable by a thin, insistent whistle or a high-pitched *kek-kek-kek*.

Habitat

Once called the Marsh Hawk, the Northern Harrier frequents wetlands and open fields.

Local Sites

Look for the Northern Harrier year-round at Piney Tract, and in grasslands near Yellow Creek State Park, north of Moraine State Park, and south of Shenango Reservoir.

FIELD NOTES A Northern Harrier gliding high overhead can look like a falcon, due to its long, broad tail. Look for the bright white on the Northern Harrier's rump, one of the most noticeable field marks of any of the hawk species.

Juvenile

COOPER'S HAWK

Accipiter cooperii L 14-20" (36-51 cm) WS 29-37" (74-94 cm)

FIELD MARKS

Blue-gray upperparts; reddish bars across breast, belly

Dark gray cap; bright red eyes

Long, rounded, barred tail with white terminal band

Juvenile brown with yellow eyes

Behavior

Scans for prey from a perch, then attacks with a sudden burst of speed. Also scans for prey while soaring. Flies fast and close to the ground, using brush to conceal its rapid attack. Typically feeds on birds, rabbits, rodents, reptiles, and insects. Known to hold prey underwater to drown it. Gives a high *kew-kew-kew* call at nest site.

Habitat

Prefers broken, especially deciduous, woodlands and streamside groves. Has adapted to fragmented woodlands created by urban and suburban development.

Local Sites

These birds nest and hunt in open woodlands year-round, and at bird feeders in urban and suburban yards in winter. They commonly migrate past hawk lookouts along the Kittatinny Ridge.

FIELD NOTES Distinguishing a Cooper's from a Sharp-shinned Hawk, *Accipiter striatus* (inset: juvenile, left; adult, right), is one of birding's more difficult identifications. Both species are largely brown as juveniles; blue-gray above, barred rufous below as adults. The Sharp-shinned is slightly smaller, has a squared-off tail, and its neck does not extend as far out in flight.

Year-round | Adult

RED-SHOULDERED HAWK

Buteo lineatus L 15-19" (38-48 cm) WS 37-42" (94-107 cm)

FIELD MARKS
Adult has reddish shoulders and
wing linings; pale spotting above

Breast barred reddish with dark
streaks; head has a grayish cast

In flight, shows black tail with
white bands and a pale crescent
at base of primaries

Behavior
Flies with several wing beats, followed by a glide on
flattened wings. Look for it during fall migration, sav-
ing its energy by soaring on rising currents of warm
air, called thermals. Hunts from low perches for snakes,
amphibians, small mammals, and an occasional small
bird. Nests close to tree trunks, 10 to 200 feet up.
Returns to the same territory for years, sometimes even
passing nests along to succeeding generations. Call is
an evenly spaced series of clear, high *KEE-ahh* notes.

Habitat
Prefers woodlands, especially moist, mixed woods near
water and swamps.

Local Sites
These birds breed in forests, woodlands, marshlands,
and even in urban and suburban areas across the state,
but they are most easily seen as fall migrants at Hawk
Mountain Sanctuary on Kittatinny Ridge.

FIELD NOTES Five subspecies of Red-shouldered Hawk occur
regularly in North America. The widespread eastern race,
lineatus (pictured opposite), is characterized by a brown-
streaked rufous chest. The immature of this subspecies has
brown upperparts, and a finely streaked brown and white breast.

Year-round | Adult light morph

BROAD-WINGED HAWK

Buteo platypterus L 16" (41 cm) WS 34" (86 cm)

FIELD MARKS
Dark brown above; adult pale
below with rufous barring;
immature darkly streaked below

In flight, white underwings have
dark borders

Short, broad tail has black and
white bands

Behavior
In fall, migrates in large flocks, called kettles, often
composed of thousands of birds. Perches near water at
the edge of woods, then swoops down on its prey of
amphibians, reptiles, rodents, small birds, and large
insects. Nests of the Broad-winged, composed of sticks,
leaves, bark, and lichen, are built in trees by both the
male and female in a process which can last up to five
weeks. Its call is a thin, shrill, slightly descending whistle of *kee-eee*, easily imitated by Blue Jays.

Habitat
Breeds in deciduous forests of the eastern woodlands of
North America. Winters primarily in the Amazon River
region of South America.

Local Sites
Look for Broad-wingeds in any wooded area during the
breeding season. Better yet, watch them migrate south
along the Kittatinny Ridge in late August and September—sometimes thousands in a single day—at Hawk
Mountain Sanctuary.

FIELD NOTES A long-distance migrant, this smallest of the
eastern buteos will avoid long water crossings as much as
possible. Instead, it will follow inland mountain ridges, gliding
upon energy-saving updrafts of air along the ridges.

Year-round | Adult

RED-TAILED HAWK

Buteo jamaicensis L 22" (56 cm) WS 50" (127 cm)

FIELD MARKS

Brown above; red tail on adults

Whitish belly with broad band of dark streaking

Dark bar on leading edge of underwing

Immature has brown, banded tail

Behavior

Watch for the Red-tailed Hawk circling above, searching for rodents, sometimes kiting, or hanging motionless on the wind. Uses thermals to gain lift and limit its energy expenditure while soaring. Perches for long intervals on telephone poles and other man-made structures, often in urban areas. Nests in large trees, on cliffs, or on man-made structures; often uses old nests abandoned by other hawks. Listen for its distinctive call, a harsh, rising then descending *shee-eeee-arr.*

Habitat

Found in a variety of habitats from woods to prairies to farmland, and even in urban settings. Common at habitat edges, where field meets forest or wetlands meet woodlands, favored for the variety of prey found there.

Local Sites

Pennsylvania's most common resident hawk is conspicuous at all seasons when perched along roadsides and circling above highways throughout the state.

FIELD NOTES While perched, Red-taileds are easy to spot, but when migrating, the hawks soar at altitudes up to 5,000 feet, appearing as nothing more than specks in the sky.

Year-round | Adult male

AMERICAN KESTREL

Falco sparverius L 10.5" (27 cm) WS 23" (58 cm)

FIELD MARKS
Russet back and tail; streaked
tawny to pale underparts

Two black stripes on white face

Male has blue-gray wing coverts

Female has russet wing coverts
and russet streaks on her breast

Behavior
Feeds on insects, reptiles, mice and other small
mammals. Hovers over prey, then plunges down for the
kill. Will also feed on small birds, especially in winter.
Regularly seen perched on fences and telephone lines,
bobbing its tail with frequency. Nests in tree holes,
barns, or man-made boxes using little or no nesting
material. Has clear, shrill call of *killy-killy-killy* or *klee-
klee-klee*, given year-round.

Habitat
North America's most widely distributed falcon, found
in open country and in cities, often mousing along
highway medians or sweeping along riparian areas.

Local Sites
Though declining in numbers, this smallest falcon is
still a fairly common breeder throughout Pennsylvania.
Hundreds of migrants pass Hawk Mountain Sanctuary,
Waggoner's Gap, and other lookouts on the Kittattinny
Ridge each autumn.

FIELD NOTES The kestrel population of Pennsylvania is threatened by factors such as competition for nesting holes with the
introduced European Starling and an increasing amount of farmland being given over to forest. Where farming is still plentiful,
such as Pennsylvania Dutch country, so are the kestrels.

Year-round | Immature

PEREGRINE FALCON

Falco peregrinus L 16-20" (41-51 cm) WS 36-44" (91-112 cm)

FIELD MARKS

Blue-black crown and nape

Black extends below eye, forming distinctive "helmet"

Adult shows rufous wash below

Juvenile is brownish above; underparts heavily streaked

Behavior

This incredibly fast raptor hunts by flying high on powerful wingbeats, then swooping in on prey in a spectacular dive that can clock in at 175 mph or more. Also flies low over water to surprise waterfowl prey. Feeds primarily on birds, the larger of which may be knocked out of the air and subsequently eaten on the ground. Nests on cliffs, bridges, or tall buildings with very little nesting material. Though usually silent, gives out loud *kak-kak-kak* call at nesting area.

Habitat

Traditionally breeds near cliffs; but now also established in cities. Hunts a wide area and in a variety of habitats.

Local Sites

These spectacular raptors are fairly easy to see near their nests on center-city buildings in Pittsburgh and Harrisburg and on at least six Delaware River bridges in the Philadelphia area.

FIELD NOTES The Merlin, *Falco columbarius* (inset: male, left; female, right), is another fast, powerful, and aggressive falcon that visits Pennsylvania primarily on migration. It is smaller than the Peregrine and lacks the Peregrine's distinctive "helmeted" look.

Year-round | Adult

AMERICAN COOT

Fulica americana L 15.5" (39 cm)

FIELD MARKS
Blackish head; slate gray body

Small, reddish brown forehead shield; reddish eyes on adult

Whitish bill with dark band at tip; greenish legs with lobed toes

Juvenile paler with darker bill

Behavior
The coot's distinctive toes are flexible and lobed, permitting it to swim well and to dive for aquatic vegetation and invertebrates. Runs on water, flapping wings rapidly to gain momentum to take flight. Bobs its small head back and forth when walking or swimming. Forages in large flocks, especially during winter. Makes a floating nest anchored to aquatic vegetation. Has a wide vocabulary of grunts, cackles, and chatter.

Habitat
Breeds in freshwater marshes or on lakes and ponds. Winters on both fresh and salt water. The coot has also adapted to human-altered habitats, including sewage lagoons for foraging and suburban lawns for roosting.

Local Sites
Breeds sparingly at Geneva Marsh and Erie National Wildlife Refuge. Large flocks migrate through Presque Isle, Moraine, and Yellow Creek State Parks, the lower Susquehanna River, and John Heinz National Wildlife Refuge.

FIELD NOTES The Common Moorhen, *Gallinula chloropus* (inset), inhabits many of the same freshwater wetlands as the coot. It has a bright red forehead shield which extends onto a red bill tipped with yellow.

Year-round | Adult

KILLDEER

Charadrius vociferus L 10.5" (27 cm)

FIELD MARKS

Gray-brown above; white neck
and belly; two black breast bands

Black stripe on forehead and one
extending back from black bill

Red-orange rump visible in flight

Red orbital ring

Behavior

Often seen running, then stopping on a dime with an
inquisitive look, then suddenly jabbing at the ground
with its bill. Feeds mainly on insects that live in short
vegetation. May gather in loose flocks, but more often
seen by itself. Builds its nest on about any spot of
open ground, even in residential areas. Listen for the
Killdeer's loud, piercing, eponymous call of *kill-dee* or
its rising *dee-dee-dee*. Also gives a long, trilled *trrrrrrr*
during courtship display or when its nest is threatened
by a predator.

Habitat

Although a type of plover—one of the shorebirds—the
Killdeer prefers inland grassy regions, but may also be
found on shores.

Local Sites

Noisy and active, the abundant Killdeer is easy to find
in fields, pastures, golf courses, urban parks, and at the
edges of lakes and ponds.

FIELD NOTES If its nest is threatened by an intruder, the Killdeer is
known to feign a broken wing, limping to one side, dragging its
wing, and spreading its tail in an attempt to lure the threat away
from its young. Once the predator is far enough away from the
nest, the instantly "healed" Killdeer takes flight.

Nonbreeding | Adult

GREATER YELLOWLEGS

Tringa melanoleuca L 14" (36 cm)

FIELD MARKS
Long, dark, slightly upturned bill;
long, bright yellow-orange legs

Head and neck streaked gray-
brown; white-speckled, gray-
brown back

In breeding season: white underparts barred gray-brown on flanks

Behavior
A forager of snails, crabs, and shrimp; also skims
surface of water for insects and larvae. Sprints short
distances in pursuit of small fish. Usually seen alone or
in small groups, this wary bird sounds an alarm when a
hawk or falcon approaches. Call is distinctive series of
three or more loud, repeated, descending *tew-tew-tew*
notes, heard most often in flight.

Habitat
In migration, frequents a full range of wetlands, including marshes, ponds, lakes, rivers, and reservoirs. Breeds
across the Canadian boreal zone.

Local Sites
Mud flats, shallow marshes, and wet fields at
Pymatuning State Park, along the Lower Susquehanna
River, and at John Heinz National Wildlife Refuge host
migrants in spring and fall.

FIELD NOTES The Lesser Yellowlegs, *Tringa flavipes*, is a closely
related and almost identically plumaged shorebird. It shares
much of the Greater's winter habitat. Distinguished by its shorter,
straighter bill—about the length of its head—it is smaller in
stature and less wary in behavior. The Lesser's call is higher and
shorter, consisting of one or two *tew* notes. It begins its migration later than the Greater, but can be observed in the same
locales, especially John Heinz National Wildlife Refuge.

Breeding | Adult

SPOTTED SANDPIPER

Actitis macularia L 7.5" (19 cm)

FIELD MARKS
Olive-brown upperparts, barred
during breeding season

White underparts, spotted brown
while breeding

Short, straight orange bill tipped
in black; short white wing stripe
in flight

Behavior
Often seen singly, feeding on insects, crustaceans, and
other invertebrates by plucking them from the water's
surface or snatching them from the air. Walks with a
constant teetering motion. Flies with stiff, shallow
wingbeats. The slightly larger female is the first to
establish territory and to defend it during breeding season. Nests on grass near water. Calls include a shrill
peet-weet and a series of *weet* notes, given in flight.

Habitat
Inhabits sheltered ponds, lakes, streams, and marshes.

Local Sites
These birds are rather uncommon breeders but com-
mon migrants throughout the state. Look for them at
Pymatuning State Park, on the lower Susquehanna
River, and at John Heinz National Wildlife Refuge.

FIELD NOTES Another regular migrant across the state, the Solitary Sandpiper, *Tringa solitaria* (inset:
breeding), has a longer neck than the
Spotted; its lower throat, breast, and sides
are streaked blackish brown; its brown
upperparts are heavily spotted buffy white;
and it has a bold white eye ring. Its call is
higher pitched and more emphatic.

Nonbreeding | Adult

LEAST SANDPIPER

Calidris minutilla L 6" (15 cm)

FIELD MARKS
Short, thin, slightly decurved bill
Gray-brown upperparts
Streaked gray-brown breast band
White belly and undertail coverts
Yellowish to greenish legs

Behavior
Forages for food with its short, spiky bill. Feeds on worms, insects, mollusks, small crabs, and fish, in muddy, sandy, or shallow water. Not wary of humans, it will investigate picnic sites on beaches. If flushed, flies off rapidly in a zigzag flight pattern. The Least Sandpiper's call is a high *kree* or *jeet*.

Habitat
Found in tidal coastal regions and wetlands with exposed mud or sand. Breeds in the Arctic.

Local Sites
Strictly migrants, these tiny shorebirds rest and feed in large flocks between April and May and between August and September along the lower Susquehanna River; at John Heinz National Wildlife Refuge; and, in years when low water levels produce mudflats, at Shenango Reservoir.

FIELD NOTES The most diminutive of shorebirds collectively known as "peeps," the Least Sandpiper's yellow-green legs set it apart from the slightly larger Semipalmated Sandpiper, *Calidris pusilla*, which has black legs. The Least's bill is also slightly downcurved—the Semipalmated's is straight—and its breast band is more pronounced. These two peeps follow many of the same migration routes through Pennsylvania.

Year-round | Adult

AMERICAN WOODCOCK

Scolopax minor L 11" (28 cm)

FIELD MARKS
Chunky; mottled brown and gray
above and orange-brown below

Long, stout bill

Short neck, legs, and tail

Large eyes set high in the head

Rounded wings

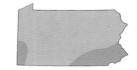

Behavior
This secretive bird is most often spotted at dusk. It uses
its long bill to probe deep into the damp earth of the
forest floor for its favorite meal of earthworms. Also
eats millipedes, beetles, and flies. Its flexible upper bill
tip allows it to snatch prey below ground. If flushed, it
will fly up abruptly, its wings making a loud, twittering
sound. Its nasal *peent* is heard mainly in spring.

Habitat
Although a shorebird, the American Woodcock prefers
moist woodlands, where it nests on the forest floor.

Local Sites
Though their population is declining, the woodcock can
be found by searching carefully in any moist, shrubby
field or open woodland. Look for it at Presque Isle and
Moraine State Parks, and Erie and John Heinz National
Wildlife Refuges, especially in early spring.

FIELD NOTES The slightly smaller Wilson's Snipe,
Gallinago delicata (inset), has a long bill for
probing the mud of wetlands. It has a boldly
striped head and barred flanks. In swooping
display flights, its vibrating outer tail
feathers make quavering hoots.

Breeding | Adult

BONAPARTE'S GULL

Larus philadelphia L 13.5" (34 cm) WS 33" (84 cm)

FIELD MARKS

Breeding adult has black hood, absent in winter adult

Gray mantle and upperwings

Black-and-white wingtips, pale on underside; white underparts

Black bill; orange-red legs

Behavior

Among the smallest and most graceful of North American gulls. Though it is omnivorous and willing to forage on a variety of prey, it seldom feeds at garbage dumps, unlike most other gulls. Often forages in large flocks, and will gather at river mouths, diving for small fish and wading for fish eggs. Gives low, raspy chatters and single *mew* calls.

Habitat

Favors marine environments during winter, but stops off at lakes, ponds, rivers, and marshes on migration. Breeds in coniferous forests of Canada and Alaska.

Local Sites

Presque Isle State Park hosts many thousands of migrants annually, especially in autumn. Other migration hot spots are Pymatuning State Park and the lower Susquehanna and Delaware Rivers.

FIELD NOTES Most birds on spring migration show the full black hood of the breeding adult (pictured opposite), but on fall migration, look for the less distinct dark spots behind the eyes of the winter adult (inset). Immature Bonaparte's Gulls show some brown on wings and a dark tail band.

Year-round | Adult

RING-BILLED GULL

Larus delawarensis L 17.5" (45 cm) WS 48" (122 cm)

FIELD MARKS

Yellow bill with black subterminal
ring; pale eye with dark orbital ring

Pale gray upperparts; white
underparts; yellowish legs; black
primaries show white spots

Head streaked light brown in winter

Behavior

This opportunistic feeder will scavenge for garbage,
grains, dead fish, fruit, and marine invertebrates. A
vocal gull, it calls, croaks, and cries incessantly,
especially during feeding. The call consists of a series of
laughing croaks that begins with a short, gruff note
and falls into a series of *kheeyaahhh* sounds.

Habitat

Common along shorelines in winter, but also a regular
visitor to most inland bodies of water, especially
reservoirs in urban areas.

Local Sites

Thousands spend the winter on the lower Susquehanna
and Delaware Rivers, as well as at Presque Isle when the
water is ice free. Migrating Ring-billeds are common
on rivers and lakes statewide, and they often stop in
fast-food parking lots for a quick meal.

FIELD NOTES The Ring-billed along with its
partner in crime, the Herring Gull, *Larus
argentatus* (inset: nonbreeding), are the two
quintessential "seagulls." Adults are similar in
plumage color and pattern, but the Herring
Gull is noticeably larger with a red spot on its
lower mandible and pinkish legs.

Year-round | Adult

GREAT BLACK-BACKED GULL

Larus marinus L 30" (76 cm) WS 65" (165 cm)

FIELD MARKS

Large gull; adult has large yellow
bill with red spot on lower
mandible

Black mantle and upper wing;
white head, neck, and underparts

White primary tips, tail, and
uppertail coverts; pink legs

Behavior

The largest gull in the world, the Great Black-backed
will bully smaller gulls and take their lunches. Also
scavenges on beaches for mollusks, crustaceans, insects,
and eggs; wades in water for fish, roots through garbage
for carrion and refuse, and even kills birds as large as
cormorants. On breeding grounds, listen for a low,
slow *keeeeyaaaahh*.

Habitat

Coastal areas of eastern North America and large
inland lakes and rivers. Breeding range is extending
southward along the Atlantic coast.

Local Sites

Great Black-backed gulls commonly migrate and winter at Presque Isle State Park and on the lower Delaware
and Susquehanna Rivers.

FIELD NOTES The Lesser Black-backed Gull, *Larus
fuscus* (inset: nonbreeding), is actually dark gray on
its back and wings and resembles the Herring Gull,
Larus argentatus, but is darker above and has yellow
legs. With numbers steadily increasing, the
Lesser Black-backeds can now be found regularly
in winter on the lower Delaware and Susquehanna Rivers.

Breeding | Adult

CASPIAN TERN

Sterna caspia L 21" (53 cm) WS 50" (127 cm)

FIELD MARKS

Large, thick, red bill with dark tip

Pale gray above, white below

Breeding adult has black cap; winter adult's crown is dusky

In flight, shows dark primary tips and slightly forked tail

Behavior

Usually solitary, often hovers before diving for small fish, its main food. Also swims gull-like and feeds from the water's surface. Largest of the terns, the Caspian frequently steals catches from other gulls and terns, and feeds on their eggs and chicks. Adult calls include a loud rasping *rraah* or *ahhrr* and a drawn-out, upslurred *rrah-ah-ahr*. Juvenile call when begging for food is a high, thin whistled *ssiiuuh*.

Habitat

Locally common and widespread on coastlines world-wide. Small colonies nest together on beaches or on islands of inland rivers.

Local Sites

Commonly migrate in spring and fall at Presque Isle and Pymatuning State Parks, and on the lower Delaware and Susquehanna Rivers.

FIELD NOTES Compare the Caspian Tern to the smaller Common Tern, *Sterna hirundo* (inset: breeding). Note the Common's red legs and thinner bill. In flight, the Common Tern's tail is noticeably more deeply forked, and the underwing tips show more white, with a thin black line extending along the trailing edge from the tip to midwing. Look for Common Terns primarily along the Lake Erie shore.

Year-round | Adult

ROCK PIGEON

Columba livia L 12.5" (32 cm)

FIELD MARKS

Variably plumaged, with head and neck usually darker than back

White cere at base of dark bill, pink legs

Iridescent feathers on neck reflect green, bronze, and purple

Behavior

Feeds on grain, seeds, fruit, and refuse; a frequent visitor to farms and backyard feeding stations. As it forages, moves with a short-stepped, "pigeon-toed" gait while its head bobs back and forth. Courtship display consists of male puffing out neck feathers, fanning tail, and turning in circles while cooing. Nests and roosts primarily on high window ledges, on bridges, and in barns. Characterized by soft *coo-cuk-cuk-cuk-cooo* call.

Habitat

Introduced from Europe in the 1600s, the Rock Pigeon is now found almost anywhere near human habitation.

Local Sites

The familiar beggar and street-cleaner is common in almost every city and town, and large flocks live in many farmyards.

FIELD NOTES The Rock Pigeon's variable colors, ranging from rust red to all white to mosaic (inset), were developed over centuries of near domestication. The pigeons that most resemble their wild ancestors have a dark head and neck, two black wing bars, a white rump, and a black terminal band on the tail.

Year-round | Adult

MOURNING DOVE

Zenaida macroura L 12" (31 cm)

FIELD MARKS

Gray-brown; black spots on upper
wings; white tips on outer tail
feathers show in flight

Trim-bodied; long pointed tail

Black spot on lower cheek;
pinkish wash on neck.

Behavior

Generally a ground feeder, the Mourning Dove forages
for grains, seeds, grasses, and insects. Like other
Columbidae, it is able to slurp up water without tipping
back its head. The Mourning Dove is aggressively territorial while nesting, but will gather into large roosting
flocks after breeding season. Also known to produce
multiple broods a season. Wings produce a fluttering
whistle as the bird takes flight. Known for its mournful
call, *oowooo-woo-woo-woo*, given by males during
breeding season.

Habitat

Widespread and abundant, the Mourning Dove is
found in a variety of habitats, but prefers open areas,
often choosing suburban sites for feeding and nesting.

Local Sites

Abundant throughout the state, these birds can be
found in virtually every habitat except deep forests.

FIELD NOTES The Mourning Dove, like other members of the
family *Columbidae*, has the ability to produce "pigeon milk" in its
crop lining. It regurgitates this substance to its young during their
first few days. In appearance and nutritious content, it is remark-
ably similar to the milk of mammals.

Year-round | Adult

YELLOW-BILLED CUCKOO

Coccyzus americanus L 12" (31 cm)

FIELD MARKS
Gray-brown above, mostly white
below; yellow orbital ring

Decurved bill with dark upper
mandible and yellow lower

Underside of tail patterned in bold
black and white

Behavior
This shy species slips quietly through woodlands,
combing vegetation for caterpillars and insects. During
courtship, male climbs on female's shoulders to feed
her from above. Builds nest of grasses and moss on
horizontal tree limb. Unique song sounds hollow and
wooden, a rapid staccato *kuk-kuk-kuk*, usually
descending to a *kakakowlp-kowlp* ending; it is often
heard just before a storm in spring and summer.

Habitat
Common in dense canopies of woods, orchards, and
streamside groves. Also inhabits tangles of swamp
edges. Winters in South America.

Local Sites
Look high in trees—or better yet, listen for these birds'
calls—in any woodland. Moraine and Ryerson Station
State Parks, the State College and Huntingdon areas,
and rural lands near the lower Susquehanna River are
among the best spots.

FIELD NOTES The closely related Black-
billed Cuckoo, *Coccyzus erythropthalmus*
(inset), is known to sometimes lay its eggs in
the nests of Yellow-billeds. It is best distinguished by its dark bill and red eye ring.

Year-round | Adult

BARN OWL

Tyto alba L 16" (41 cm) WS 42" (107 cm)

FIELD MARKS

White heart-shaped face

Dark eyes, pale bill

Rusty brown above; cinnamon-barred wings

White to pale cinnamon spotted underparts, darker on females

Behavior

A nocturnal forager of rodents, small birds, bats, snakes, and insects. Hunts primarily by sound, often in pastures and marshes. Wing feathers with loosely knit edges and soft body plumage make its flight almost soundless—effective in surprising prey. Roosts and nests at all times of year in dark cavities in city and farm buildings, in burrows, cliff holes, and hollow trees. Song is a long, raspy, hissing shriek, often repeated.

Habitat

Distributed throughout the world, the Barn Owl is found in urban, suburban, rural, and other open regions throughout its range.

Local Sites

As old-fashioned barns have disappeared, this species has declined severely, but still nests locally in farmlands in the state's southeastern Piedmont region. Since these owls can be hard to find, a good tactic is to stop in a rural town and ask if anyone knows of a nesting site.

FIELD NOTES The Barn Owl hunts primarily by sound. With its asymmetrically placed ear openings, it can pinpoint the location of its prey even in total darkness

Year-round | Adult rufous morph

EASTERN SCREECH-OWL

Megascops asio L 8.5" (22 cm)

FIELD MARKS
Small; with yellow eyes and pale tip on yellow-green bill

Rufous and gray morphs occur

Underparts marked by vertical streaks crossed by dark bars

Ear tufts prominent if raised

Behavior
Nocturnal; uses exceptional vision and hearing to hunt for mice, voles, shrews, and insects. Seeks out densest and thickest cover available for daytime roost and, if approached, will stretch its body, erect its ear tufts, and shut its eyes to blend into background. Nests in tree cavities about 10 to 30 feet up. Emits a series of quavering trills, descending in pitch, when defending territory; and a long, low-pitched trill around the nest site.

Habitat
Found in a wide variety of habitats including woodlots, forests, swamps, parks, and suburban gardens.

Local Sites
Most urban parks, even in large cities such as Pittsburgh and Philadelphia, have resident populations that are easy to find. You will often hear a response or lure a screech-owl into view by imitating its call in any area with small woodlots surrounded by open space.

FIELD NOTES Pennsylvania's smallest owl, only about the size of a robin, the Northern Saw-whet, *Aegolius acadicus* (inset), is difficult to study due to its elusive nature and diminutive size. Recent surveys show that Saw-whets are more common in the state than peviously thought, and banding programs indicate that fairly large numbers migrate through central Pennsylvania.

Year-round | Adult

GREAT HORNED OWL

Bubo virginianus L 22" (56 cm) WS 54" (137 cm)

FIELD MARKS

Mottled brownish gray above, densely barred below

Long ear tufts, or "horns"

Rust-colored facial disks

Yellow eyes; white chin and throat; buff-colored underwings

Behavior

Chiefly nocturnal. Watches from perch, then swoops down on prey, which includes cats, skunks, porcupines, birds, snakes, rodents, and frogs. Reuses abandoned nests of other large birds. Begins nesting by February, possibly to take advantage of winter-stressed prey. Territorial song, often sung in duet, consists of three to eight loud, deep hoots, the second and third often short and rapid. Song mostly heard at dusk and dawn.

Habitat

The most widespread owl in North America, the Great Horned Owl can be found in a wide variety of habitats including forests, cities, and farmlands.

Local Sites

Common throughout the state, listen for a Great Horned's call in any woodland. Erie National Wildlife Refuge and Bald Eagle, Ricketts Glen, and Beltzville State Parks are all likely spots.

FIELD NOTES Only slightly smaller than the Great Horned, the Barred Owl, *Strix varia* (inset), also inhabits a variety of woodlands in Pennsylvania. Its loud rhythmic call, *who-cooks-for-you, who-cooks-for-you-all*, is much more likely to be heard during the day than most owls' calls.

Year-round | Adult

COMMON NIGHTHAWK

Chordeiles minor L 9.5" (24 cm)

FIELD MARKS

Dark gray-brown mottled back;
bold white bar across primaries

Long, pointed wings with pale
spotting; tail slightly forked

Underparts whitish with bold
dusky bars; bar on tail in males

Behavior

Hunts in flight, snaring insects; streamlined body
allows agile aerial maneuvers. Drops lower jaw to
create opening wide enough to take in even large
moths. Skims over surface of lakes to drink. Roosts on
the ground and on branches, posts, or roofs. Nests on
the ground or on gravel rooftops. Male's wings make
hollow booming sound during diving courtship
display. Male gives a nasal *peent* in flight.

Habitat

Frequents woodlands, shrubby areas, and urban and
suburban settings. Winters in South America.

Local Sites

Numbers have declined, but these birds can still be seen
at dusk overhead in many cities and towns. In late
August and early September, sit along the Allegheny,
Susquehanna, and Delaware Rivers to see dozens or
even hundreds passing in their fall migration.

FIELD NOTES Another nighttime insect hunter of summer, the
Whip-poor-will, *Caprimulgus vociferus* (inset),
hunts in flight for moths and mosquitoes
and roosts on the ground during the day. It
is most easily identified in the field by its
loud, melodious song: *WHIP poor WILL*.

Year-round | Adult

CHIMNEY SWIFT

Chaetura pelagica L 5.3" (13 cm)

FIELD MARKS
Short, cigar-shaped body
Long, pointed, narrow wings
Dark plumage, sooty gray overall
Short, stubby tail
Blackish gray bill, legs, feet

Behavior
Crisscrosses the sky with rapid wing beats of long wings at impressive speeds, snatching up ants, termites, and spiders while in flight. Look for large groups of migrating Chimney Swifts circling above rooftops at dusk before dropping into chimneys or steeples to roost. Builds cup-shaped nest of small twigs glued together with dried saliva in chimneys, under eaves of barns, and in hollow trees. During aerial courtship, the male raises his wings into a sharp V. Call, given in flight, is a rapid, continual, high-pitched chattering.

Habitat
Often seen soaring over forested, open, suburban, and urban areas. Winters as far south as Peru.

Local Sites
These fast fliers are abundant summer residents throughout Pennsylvania, streaking and wheeling overhead at spectacular speeds.

FIELD NOTES The Chimney Swift once confined its nests to tree hollows and other natural sites. Over the centuries, it has adapted so well to artificial nesting sites such as chimneys, air shafts, vertical pipes, barns, and silos, that the species' numbers have increased dramatically. It is the only swift seen regularly in the eastern United States.

Year-round | Adult male

RUBY-THROATED HUMMINGBIRD

Archilochus colubris L 3.8" (10 cm)

FIELD MARKS

Metallic green above

Adult male has brilliant red gorget, black chin, whitish underparts, dusky green sides

Female lacks gorget, has whitish throat and underparts, and a buffy wash on sides

Behavior

Probes backyard hummingbird feeders and flowers for nectar by hovering virtually still in midair. Also feeds on small spiders and insects. When nectar is scarce, known to drink sap from wells made in tree trunks by sapsuckers. In spring, male Ruby-throateds arrive in breeding territory before females and engage in jousts to claim prime territory. Once mated, females build nests on small tree limbs and raise young by themselves. In addition to the "hum" generated by its rapidly beating wings, this bird emits soft *tchew* notes.

Habitat

Found in gardens and woodland edges throughout most of the eastern United States.

Local Sites

There are no places better to see these tiny birds than in yards with hummingbird feeders or an abundance of flowers. Look for them throughout the summer.

FIELD NOTES Hummingbirds and the flowers they pollinate have evolved to meet each other's needs. Typical flowers favored by the birds are narrow and tubular, the nectar accessible only to a long bill or tongue. The hummingbird is attracted to the flowers' bright colors; a sign, perhaps, of the nectar within.

Juvenile | Immature male

BELTED KINGFISHER

Ceryle alcyon L 13" (33 cm)

FIELD MARKS
Blue-gray head with large,
shaggy crest

Blue-gray upperparts and breast
band; white underparts and collar

Long, heavy, black bill

Female: Chestnut sides and belly band

Behavior
Generally solitary and vocal, dives headfirst for fish from
a waterside perch or after hovering above in order to line
up on its target. Also feeds on insects, amphibians, and
small reptiles. Monogamous pairs nest in burrows they
dig together three or more feet into vertical earthen
banks near watery habitats. Both male and female share
in parenting duties as well. Mated pairs renew their
relationship each breeding season with courtship ritu-
als such as dramatic display flights, the male's feeding
of the female, and vocalizations. Call is a loud, dry rattle; it is given when alarmed, to announce territory, or
while in flight. Also makes harsh *caar* notes.

Habitat
Conspicuous along rivers, ponds, lakes, and coastal
estuaries. Prefers partially wooded areas.

Local Sites
Look for these birds perched on branches overhanging
the water at virtually every lake, creek, and river in the
state. Pymatuning, Moraine, Yellow Creek, Beltzville,
and Marsh Creek State Parks are all good bets.

FIELD NOTES The Belted Kingfisher female is one of the few in
North America that is more colorful than her male counterpart,
which lacks the female's chestnut band across the belly and
chestnut sides and flanks.

Year-round | Adult male

RED-BELLIED WOODPECKER

Melanerpes carolinus L 9.3" (24 cm)

FIELD MARKS
Black-and-white barred back

Red nape, extending onto crown only on males

Mostly grayish underparts; small reddish tinge on belly

Central tail feathers barred

Behavior
Climbs tree trunks by bracing itself with stiff tail, taking strain off short legs. Uses chisel-shaped bill to drill cavities in tree bark for nest holes and to extract grubs and insects. Also feeds on worms, fruits, seeds, and sap. Will visit backyard feeders for sunflower seeds and peanut butter. Nests and roosts at night in tree cavities. Call during breeding season is a rolling *churrr*. Also gives a conversational *chiv chiv* all year.

Habitat
Common in open woodlands, forest edges, suburbs, and parks.

Local Sites
These conspicuous residents are common in cities, suburbs, parks, and woodlands throughout the western and southeastern counties of Pennsylvania.

FIELD NOTES The Red-headed Woodpecker, *Melanerpes erythrocephalus* (inset: adult, left; juvenile, right), shares much of the Red-bellied's range, but is much less common. The adult Red-headed is identified by its bright red hood and its stark white rump and underparts. The juvenile has a brownish hood and back.

Year-round | Adult male

YELLOW-BELLIED SAPSUCKER

Sphyrapicus varius L 8.5" (22 cm)

FIELD MARKS

Red forecrown on black-and-white head; chin, throat red on male, white on female

Back blackish with white barring; white rump and wing patch

Pale yellow wash on underparts

Behavior

Alone or in a pair, drills rows of evenly spaced holes in trees, then feeds on sap produced and insects attracted. Guards these wells fiercely from other birds and mammals. Also eats fruits, berries, and tree buds. Courtship ritual includes incessantly loud drumming by both male and female, *hoy-hoy* cries, and dual tapping at nest entrance. Though often silent, the Yellow-bellied sometimes makes a low, plaintive *meeww* call, or a territorial call of *quee-ark*.

Habitat

The most highly migratory of all North American woodpeckers, found in deciduous and mixed forests.

Local Sites

Allegheny National Forest, Erie National Wildlife Refuge, and the Pocono Mountains are strongholds for these birds—but search carefully because they are often quiet and inconspicuous.

FIELD NOTES The bone and muscle structure of a woodpecker's head is an effective shock absorber; a necessary adaptation for a bird that spends its time drilling into hard wood. Similarly, a stiff tail and sharp claws help to maintain the bird's upright position against a tree trunk. Notice how a woodpecker's tail braces the bird; a much needed support to maintain its vertical perches.

Year-round | Adult female

DOWNY WOODPECKER

Picoides pubescens L 6.8" (17 cm)

FIELD MARKS
Black cap, ear patch, moustachial
stripe; black wings spotted white

Blaze of white on back

White tuft in front of eyes;
whitish underparts

Red occipital patch on male

Behavior
The smallest woodpecker in North America, forages
mainly on insects, larvae, and eggs. Readily visits backyard feeders for sunflower seeds and suet. Will also
consume poison ivy berries. Small size enables the
Downy to forage on very small, thin limbs. Nests in
cavities of dead trees. Both male and female stake
territorial claims with their drumming. Call is a high-
pitched but soft *pik*. Also gives a high, accelerating
whinny, *kee-kee-kee-kee*.

Habitat
Found in suburbs, parks, and orchards, as well as
forests and woodlands.

Local Sites
The Downy is easy to find in any woodlands, even in
cities. Suet feeders attract them readily in winter.

FIELD NOTES The larger and less common Hairy
Woodpecker, *Picoides villosus* (inset: male), is similarly marked but has a bill as long as its head and a
sharper, louder, lower-pitched call. It also tends to
stay on tree trunks or larger limbs than the Downy.
Note as well the all-white outer tail feathers of the
Hairy Woodpecker; the Downy's outer tail feathers
are often spotted black.

Year-round | Adult female "Yellow-shafted"

NORTHERN FLICKER

Colaptes auratus L 12.5" (32 cm)

FIELD MARKS

White rump, yellowish underwing

Brown, barred back, cream underparts with black spotting, and black crescent bib

Gray crown, tan face, red crescent on nape, and, on male, black moustachial stripe

Behavior

Feeds mostly on the ground, foraging primarily for ants. A cavity-nesting bird, the flicker drills into almost any wooden surface, including utility poles and houses. An insectivore, the flicker is at least partially migratory, traveling in the winter in pursuit of food. Bows to its partner before engaging in courtship dance of exaggerated wing and tail movements. Call is a single, loud *klee-yer* heard year-round or a long series of *wick wick wick wick* during breeding season. The latter call is sometimes held for up to 15 seconds.

Habitat

Found in open woodlands and wooded suburban areas.

Local Sites

Attention-getters with their loud calls, these large woodpeckers are found in any woodland. Unlike most other woodpecker species, they can often be seen poking into the grass for grubs and ants on lawns.

FIELD NOTES The western, or "Red-shafted," form of Northern Flicker has pinkish underwings, a grayish face, and a red moustachial stripe on the male. These birds are accidental visitors to Pennsylvania. Hybrids may show some intermediate characteristics of both forms.

Year-round | Adult male

PILEATED WOODPECKER

Dryocopus pileatus L 16.5" (42 cm)

FIELD MARKS

Almost entirely black on back and wings when perched

Black, white, and red striped head; red "moustache" on male

Red cap extends to bill on male

Juvenile browner overall

Behavior

Drills long, distinctively rectangular holes on tree trunks, searching for beetle larvae and other insects. Also digs into ground, stumps, and fallen logs, feeding on carpenter ants, beetles, acorns, seeds, and fruit. Nests in cavities excavated in dead or live trees, sometimes utility poles. Calls include a loud *wuk* note and a long, irregularly delivered series of *kee kee kee kee*. Also known for slow, but powerfully loud, territorial drumming, which can be heard a mile or more away.

Habitat

Prefers dense, mature forests; also found in smaller woodlots and some parks.

Local Sites

Pennsylvania's largest and loudest woodpecker is traditionally a denizen of deep forests, but the Pileated is increasingly found visiting and nesting in small woodland tracts throughout the state, even in big-city parks. Allegheny National Forest has a large population.

FIELD NOTES The excavations of the Pileated are so extensive and deep that they may fell small trees. These holes can also attract other species, such as wrens and other woodpeckers, which use the large holes both for foraging and nesting.

Year-round | Adult

EASTERN PHOEBE

Sayornis phoebe L 7" (18 cm)

FIELD MARKS
Brownish gray above, darkest on head, wings, and tail; dark bill; lacks distinct wing bars

Underparts mostly white with pale olive wash on sides and breast

Fresh fall birds washed with yellow on belly

Behavior
Flicks tail constantly when perched, looking for flying insects to chase and snare in midair. Also easts small fish, berries, and fruit. Often builds delicate cup-like nest under bridges, in eaves, or in the rafters of old buildings, almost always near running water. Distinctive song is a rough, whistled *schree-dip,* followed by a descending *schree-brrr,* often repeated when male is attempting to lure a mate. Call is a sharp *tsip.*

Habitat
Found in woodlands, farmlands, and suburbs.

Local Sites
Listen for these birds' soft calls and look for them flycatching near old buildings, bridges, and other man-made structures anywhere in the state in summer. They usually arrive from wintering grounds in March and depart in October.

FIELD NOTES Though very similarly plumaged, the Eastern Phoebe is distinguished from the Eastern Wood-Pewee, *Contopus virens* (inset), by its habit of constantly pumping its tail when perched. The Wood-Pewee tends to perch motionless. In addition, the Wood-Pewee's lower mandible is a dull orange and it has two thin whitish wing bars.

Year-round | Adult

GREAT CRESTED FLYCATCHER

Myiarchus crinitus L 8" (20 cm)

FIELD MARKS

Gray face and breast contrasts
with bright yellow belly and
undertail coverts

Olive green above and on crest

Mostly rufous inner webs of
tail feathers

Behavior
Forages high in tall trees, picking insects from foliage
or snaging them in midair. During courtship, the male
chases the female near a chosen nesting cavity, which is
usually another bird's abandoned cavity or a birdbox.
Male rarely leaves a fertile female's side and defends
territory from other males in heated midair battles.
Leans forward and bobs head if agitated. Calls include
a loud, hoarse, ascending *whee-eep*, a softer *purr-it*,
and a series of *whit* notes. Sings a continuous series
of *whee-eep*s around dawn.

Habitat
Found in open deciduous and mixed woodlands,
including parks and suburbs. Winters for the most part
in Central and South America.

Local Sites
Common throughout the state in the breeding season,
these large flycatchers frequent open and semi-open
hardwood forests. Look for them especially in the Allegheny National Forest, Yellow Creek and Bald Eagle
State Parks, and throughout the Pocono Mountains.

FIELD NOTES The Great Crested Flycatcher has traditionally
decorated its nest with shed pieces of snakeskin, but these days
it will make do with cellophane, plastic wrap, and onion skins.

Year-round | Adult

EASTERN KINGBIRD

Tyrannus tyrannus L 8.5" (22 cm)

FIELD MARKS
Black head, slate gray back

White terminal band on black tail

Underparts white except for pale gray wash across breast

Orange-red crown patch visible only when displaying

Behavior
Waits on perch until it spots prey, then darts out to snare it in midair. Feeds primarily on flying insects. May also hover to pick food from foliage. Males court with erratic hovering, swooping, and circling, revealing hidden crown patch. Builds cup-shaped nest near the end of a tree branch, sometimes on a post or stump. Emits raspy *zeer* call when feeding or defending. Sings a complex, repeated series of notes and trills at dawn.

Habitat
Found in woodland clearings, farms, orchards, and field edges, usually near lakes, ponds and waterways. Winters in South America.

Local Sites
Found in summer anywhere in the state, these large flycatchers are common at Presque Isle, Pymatuning, and Ryerson Station State Parks in the west and at Marsh Creek State Park, Lake Nockamixon, and along the Delaware River in the east.

FIELD NOTES Living up to its Latin name, which means "tyrant of tyrants," the Eastern Kingbird will actively defend its nest, sometimes pecking at and even pulling feathers from the backs of hawks, crows, and vultures.

Year-round | Adult

WHITE-EYED VIREO

Vireo griseus L 5" (13 cm)

FIELD MARKS
Grayish olive above

Grey neck; underparts white with
pale yellow sides and flanks

Yellow spectacles; distinctive
white iris visible at close range

Two whitish wing bars

Behavior
Thick, slightly hooked bill is used for catching flies and
picking fruits and berries. Nest is located close to the
ground in shrub or small tree. More often heard than
seen, the White-eyed sings a loud, grating, jumbled,
five- to seven-note song, usually beginning and ending
with a sharp *chick*. The notes run together, the middle
portion seeming to mimic other birds' songs. Call is a
raspy *sheh-sheh*, often repeated.

Habitat
Prefers to conceal itself close to the ground in dense
thickets, brushy tangles, and forest undergrowth.

Local Sites
White-eyeds can be found nesting in Ryerson Station
and Ohiopyle State Parks in the west, and at Marsh
Creek State Park and the Green Lane Reservoir area in
the east.

FIELD NOTES Found in woodlands throughout Pennsylvania, the Yellow-throated
Vireo, *Vireo flavifrons* (inset), is distinguished from the White-eyed by its bright yellow
throat and chin, and at close range by its dark
iris. It also tends to forage higher in trees.

Year-round | Adult

BLUE-HEADED VIREO

Vireo solitarius L 5" (13 cm)

FIELD MARKS
Solid blue-gray hood contrasts
with white spectacles and throat

Olive or bluish back; yellow sides
and flanks sometimes greenish

Prominent wing bars and tertial
edges; white on outer tail feathers

Behavior
Most often by itself or in a pair, the Blue-headed is the
first vireo to return to its breeding grounds in spring.
Forages on branches and treetops for insects and sometimes fruit. May also give chase to a flying insect or
hover to pick one off foliage. Courtship display involves
much singing, bobbing, and showcasing of yellow flank
feathers by the male. Nests in forks of trees or bushes.
Song is similar to that of Red-eyed Vireo—composed
of short, clear notes and heard frequently throughout
the day.

Habitat
Common in mixed woodlands, where it stays primarily
in higher branches.

Local Sites
Allegheny National Forest, Bald Eagle State Park, and
World's End State Park are among this vireo's prime
strongholds in the breeding season.

FIELD NOTES Vireos as different in appearance as the Blue-
headed and Yellow-throated sometimes hybridize. The Blue-
headed was until 1997 grouped as a single species, the Solitary
Vireo, with two more westerly vireos, the Plumbeous, *Vireo
plumbeus*, and Cassin's, *Vireo cassinii*. They were split primarily
because a lack of overlap in breeding ranges keeps these birds
from frequently hybridizing.

Year-round | Adult

RED-EYED VIREO

Vireo olivaceus L 6" (15 cm)

FIELD MARKS
Blue-gray crown

White eyebrow, bordered above
and below in black

Olive back, darker wings and tail

White underparts

Ruby red eye, visible at close range

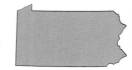

Behavior
Searches through foliage for fruits, berries, and insects,
especially caterpillars. Sometimes hovers to snatch
food from high branches. Male known to chase female
during courtship, sometimes even pinning her to the
ground. Builds nest of grass and forest debris on horizontal tree limb. Song is a variable series of deliberate,
short phrases, *cheer-o-wit, cher-ee, chit-a wit, de-o,* sung
nearly nonstop from dawn through dusk and while
brooding, foraging, roosting, and even while
swallowing. Call is a whining, down-slurred *myahh.*

Habitat
Found in the forest canopies of deciduous woodlands.

Local Sites
One of the most abundant forest birds in Pennsylvania,
Red-eyeds are common from spring through fall in
almost every wooded area in the state, even city parks.

FIELD NOTES The largely plain, grayish Warbling
Vireo, *Vireo gilvus* (inset), is best located by its
song, characterized by long, melodious, warbling
phrases delivered without pause sometimes for
hours on end. It is sung with a strong rhythm and
usually ends in an accentuated high note. Listen
for it anywhere in the state in summer, coming from
tall deciduous trees in open country near water.

Year-round | Adult

BLUE JAY

Cyanocitta cristata L 11" (28 cm)

FIELD MARKS

Blue crest and back

Black barring and white patches on blue wings and tail

Black collar line on grayish white underparts extends onto nape

Black bill, legs, and feet

Behavior

Often seen singly or in small family groups, foraging for insects, acorns and other nuts, berries, and seeds. Will also raid nests for eggs and nestlings of other species. A bobbing display may be observed during courtship. Builds nest in oak and beech trees 5 to 20 feet up. The noisy, bold Blue Jay gives a diverse array of vocalizations, including a loud, piercing alarm call of *jay jay jay,* a musical *yo-ghurt,* and imitations of several hawk species, particularly the Red-shouldered Hawk.

Habitat

Found in fragmented woodlands, parks, and suburban backyards. Some birds are migratory, while others are year-round residents.

Local Sites

Loud, flashy, and ubiquitous, the Blue Jay is common everywhere in Pennsylvania. Fall migrations of thousands of jays over Presque Isle State Park is spectacular.

FIELD NOTES A resourceful feeder, the Blue Jay will store acorns in the ground for winter months when food is scarce. As many of these acorns are never recovered, this practice is a major factor in the establishment and distribution of oak forests throughout the jay's range.

Year-round | Adult

AMERICAN CROW

Corvus brachyrhynchos L 17.5" (45 cm)

FIELD MARKS
Black, iridescent plumage overall
Broad wings and squared off tail
Long, heavy, black bill
Brown eyes
Black legs and feet

Behavior
Often forages, roosts, and travels in flocks. Individuals take turns at sentry duty while others feed on insects, garbage, grain, mice, eggs, and young birds. Known to noisily mob large raptors, such as eagles, hawks, and Great Horned Owls, in order to drive them from its territory. Because its bill is ineffective on tough hides, crows wait for another predator—or an automobile—to open a carcass before dining. Studies have shown the crow's ability to count, solve puzzles, and retain information. Nests in shrubs, trees, or on poles. Readily identified by its familiar *caw* call.

Habitat
One of North America's most widely distributed and familiar birds, lives in a variety of habitats.

Local Sites
Few species are as varied in habitat as this large "songbird," which is well-known to birders and nonbirders alike and common in forests, fields, towns, and cities.

FIELD NOTES The closely related and similarly plumaged Fish Crow, *Corvus ossifragus*, is smaller than the American Crow, but is best told apart by its high, nasal, two-syllable *ca-hah* call. It breeds in the major river valleys of eastern Pennsylvania.

Year-round | Adult

COMMON RAVEN

Corvus corax L 24" (61 cm)

FIELD MARKS

Glossy black overall with iridescent violet sheen

Long, heavy, black bill with long nasal bristles on upper mandible

Thick, shaggy throat feathers

Wedge-shaped tail

Behavior

Forages on a variety of food, from worms and insects to rodents and eggs to carrion and refuse. Small groups are known to hunt together in order to overcome prey that is too large for just one bird to take. Monogamous for life, these birds engage in acrobatic courtship flights of synchronized dives, chases, and tumbles. Builds nest high up in trees or on cliffs. Calls are variable, but include a low, drawn out *kraaah* and a nasal *brooonk*.

Habitat

Found in a variety of habitats, but most abundant in forested areas at high elevations.

Local Sites

Once mostly confined to the state's mountains and northern counties, the raven seems to be expanding slowly into lowlands east and west of the ridges. Look for it in Allegheny National Forest, Susquehannock State Forest, Bald Eagle and World's End State Parks.

FIELD NOTES The raven is considerably larger than the crow, but this can be difficult to discern from a distance. Look for the raven's wedge-shaped tail, as opposed to the squared-off tail of the crow. The raven is also much more likely to soar on flattened wings than the crow, which flies with steady wing beats.

Year-round | Adult male

HORNED LARK

Eremophila alpestris L 6.8-7.8" (17-20 cm)

FIELD MARKS

White or yellowish forehead bordered by black band, which ends in hornlike tufts on adult males

Black cheek stripes, bill, and bib

Yellow or white throat and underparts; brown or rufous upperparts

Behavior

The only lark native to North America, forages on the ground mainly on seeds, grain, and some insects. The Horned Lark walks or runs, rather than hops, and it seldom alights on trees or bushes. Outside breeding season, these birds organize into flocks. Uses its bill and feet with long hind claws to create shallow depressions for nesting. Song begins with 2 or 3 *chit* notes, then flows into a rapid, jumbled twittering that rises slightly in pitch. Calls include a high-pitched *tsee-titi*.

Habitat

Found in open agricultural fields, grasslands, dirt fields, sod farms, airports, gravel ridges, and shores.

Local Sites

Found irregularly and locally year-round in farmlands and reclaimed strip-mine grasslands, Horned Larks are particularly common at the Piney Tract Game Lands in Clarion County.

FIELD NOTES The male Horned Lark performs a spectacular flight display, ascending several hundred feet, circling and singing for a bit, then plummeting headfirst toward the ground, flaring his wings open for landing at the last second. With horns upraised, he then struts for the female, having proven his aerial agility.

Year-round | Adult male

PURPLE MARTIN

Progne subis L 8" (20 cm)

FIELD MARKS

Male is dark, glossy purplish blue

Female has bluish gray upperparts; grayish breast and belly

Long, pointed wings; forked tail

Dark eyes, bill, legs, and feet

Juvenile brown above, gray below

Behavior

Forages almost exclusively in flight, darting for wasps,
bees, dragonflies, winged ants, and other large insects.
Long, sharply pointed wings and substantial tail allow
it graceful maneuverability in the air. Capable of
drinking, even bathing, in flight by skimming just over
water's surface and dipping bill, or breast, into water.
Nests almost exclusively in man-made multi-dwelling
martin houses. Song is a series of croaks and gurgles.

Habitat

Found in open areas near martin houses and water.
Winters in South America.

Local Sites

Look for large colonies of martins nesting in the
summer at Pymatuning and Moraine State Parks in the
west and throughout the Amish farm country near the
lower Susquehanna River in the east.

FIELD NOTES Purple Martins in eastern North America are highly
dependent on man-made nesting houses, which can hold many
pairs of breeding adults. The tradition of making martin houses
from hollowed gourds originated with Native Americans, who
found that this sociable bird helped reduce insects around vil-
lages and crops. The practice was adopted by colonists, and
martins have accordingly prospered for many generations.

Year-round | Adult

TREE SWALLOW

Tachycineta bicolor L 5.8" (15 cm)

FIELD MARKS
Dark, glossy, greenish blue above

White below

Slightly notched tail

Long, pointed, blackish wings

Juvenile gray-brown above with
dusky wash on its breast

Behavior
During migration, seen in huge flocks or perched in
long rows on branches and wires. Darts over fields or
water to catch insects in flight, but switches to diet of
berries and plant buds during colder months, when
insects are less abundant. Nests in tree cavities, fence
posts, barn eaves, and man-made birdhouses. Song is a
rapid, extended series of variable chirping notes—*chrit,
pleet, euree, cheet, chrit, pleet.*

Habitat
Found in wooded habitats near water, or where dead
trees provide nest holes in fields, marshes, or towns.

Local Sites
The abundant and communal Tree Swallow nests on
lakes and ponds everywhere in the state. Presque Isle
and Pymatuning State Parks in the west, and Beltzville
and Marsh Creek State Parks in the east are good places
to find it in spring, summer, and fall.

FIELD NOTES Among the world's swallows, the Tree Swallow
more regularly feeds on plant material and has a particular
fondness for waxy bayberries, for which it has developed a
special digesting ability. These adaptations allow it to migrate
north earlier than other swallows and linger later in the fall.

Year-round | Adult

Stelgidopteryx serripennis L 5" (13 cm)

FIELD MARKS
Plain brown above with darker
wings and slightly paler rump

White below with a brownish
wash on throat and breast

Juvenile has a rusty throat and
two cinnamon wing bars

Behavior
Mostly seen singly or in pairs, except in migration
when flocks form. Flies low over open fields and water,
snagging insects in flight. May also pick insects from
water's surface. Male suitor chases female during
courtship. Traditionally digs nesting burrows in
riparian areas, but has also adapted to cavities under
bridges and highway overpasses, and in drainage culverts, for nesting. Calls include a series of low-pitched,
upwardly inflected *brrt* notes, a buzzy *jrrr-jrrr-jrrr-jrrr*,
and a higher-pitched *brzzzzzt*.

Habitat
Found in summer anywhere near water, especially
where steep banks of loose soil occur.

Local Sites
Pymatuning State Park, Shenango Reservoir, and farmlands east and west of the lower Susquehanna River
host many Rough-wingeds in the breeding season.

FIELD NOTES Often found breeding colonially in the
same exposed sandbanks as kingfishers and Northern Rough-wingeds, the Bank Swallow, *Riparia riparia*
(inset), is distinguished by its distinct brown breast
band. It also beats its wings more quickly than the
Northern Rough-winged as it flits about over its nesting tunnel, dug five to six feet into the sand.

Year-round | Adult

BARN SWALLOW

Hirundo rustica L 6.8" (17 cm)

FIELD MARKS

Long, deeply forked, dark tail

Iridescent deep blue upperparts; cinnamon to whitish underparts, paler on female

Rusty brown forehead and throat; dark blue-black breast band

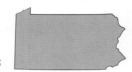

Behavior
An exuberant flyer, often seen in small flocks skimming low over the surface of a field or pond, taking insects in midair. Will follow tractors and lawn mowers to feed on flushed insects. An indicator of coming storms, as barometric pressure changes cause the bird to fly lower to the ground. Has adapted to humans to the extent that it now nests almost exclusively in structures such as barns, bridges, culverts, and garages. Call in flight is a high-pitched, squeaky *chee-jit*. Song is a long series of squeaky warbles interrupted by nasal, grating rattles.

Habitat
Frequents open farms and fields, especially those near water. Widely distributed all over the world.

Local Sites
Virtually every farm in the state hosts a colony of these abundant swallows in barns and storage buildings during the summer breeding season.

FIELD NOTES The Cliff Swallow, *Petrochelidon pyrrhonota* (inset), can also be found in summer nesting under bridges and eaves or foraging over fields and ponds. In flight, it is best distinguished from the Barn Swallow by its squarish tail and buffy rump. Its pale forehead is a distinctive field mark as well.

Year-round | Adult

BLACK-CAPPED CHICKADEE

Poecile atricapillus L 5.3" (13 cm)

FIELD MARKS
Black cap and bib

White cheeks

Grayish upperparts

Whitish underparts with rich buffy
flanks, more pronounced in fall

Wing feathers edged in white

Behavior

A common backyard bird, often the first to find a
new bird feeder. Also forages along branches and
probes bark of various trees. Diet varies seasonally,
mostly insects in sumer, more seeds and berries in
winter. Builds its nest in cavities in rotting wood or
seeks out man-made nest box. Call sounds like *chick-a-
dee-dee-dee.* Song is a variable, clear, whistled *fee-bee* or
fee-bee-ee, the first note higher in pitch.

Habitat

Common in open woodlands, clearings, and suburbs.

Local Sites

Nearly every forest, woodland, suburban area, and
urban park except in the southwestern and southeastern portions of the state is a year-round home for
these active and vocal little birds.

FIELD NOTES The Carolina Chickadee, *Poecile carolinensis* (inset), is very similar to the
Black-capped. Look for the Carolina's grayer
cheeks and grayish, rather than white, edging on
its greater coverts. Its call is also usually higher-
pitched and more rapid, a distinction that can be obscured
where the two species meet and often hybridize in
soutwestern and southeastern portions of Pennsylvania.

Year-round | Adult

TUFTED TITMOUSE

Baeolophus bicolor L 6.3" (16 cm)

FIELD MARKS

Gray above, whitish below

Russet wash on sides

Gray crest; blackish forehead

Pale spots around dark eyes

Juvenile has gray forehead and paler crest

Behavior

Very active forager in trees, seeking insects, spiders, snails, berries, and seeds. Known to hold a nut with its feet and pound it open with its bill. A common visitor to backyard feeders, especially fond of sunflower seeds and suet. Male feeds female in courtship. Nests in natural cavities, woodpecker holes, man-made boxes, and sometimes in fence posts. Song is a loud, whistled *peto-peto-peto* or *wheedle-wheedle-wheedle*. Employs up to ten different calls, including a harsh *zhee zhee zhee*, which it uses to keep foraging groups together.

Habitat

Found in open forests, woodlands, groves, and orchards, as well as urban and suburban parks.

Local Sites

These lively chatterers are easy to find year-round in forests, woodlands, and suburban parks everywhere in the state, although they are least common across the northern tier of counties.

FIELD NOTES Unintimidated by proximity to humans, the Tufted Titmouse will approach people who make a squeaking sound or *pish*, a useful tool for a birder. It is even known to swoop down and pluck hair directly from a human's scalp for use in its nest.

Year-round | Adult

WHITE-BREASTED NUTHATCH

Sitta carolinensis L 5.8" (15 cm)

FIELD MARKS
White face and breast; black cap

Blue-gray upperparts; wing and
tail feathers tipped in white

Rust or brown colored underparts
near legs

White pattern on blue-black tail

Behavior
Creeps down tree trunks or large branches in search of
insects and spiders. Will also gather nuts and seeds, jam
them into bark, and hammer or "hatch" the food open
with bill. Roosts in tree cavities, and sometimes even in
crevices of bark in summer. Builds nest in abandoned
woodpecker holes or in natural cavities inside decaying
trees. Song is a rapid series of nasal whistles on one
pitch: *whi-whi-whi-whi-whi-whi*. Call is a slow, low-
pitched, nasal *yank, yank*.

Habitat
Found in deciduous or mixed woods.

Local Sites
These upside-down tree climbers are
present year-round in large forests,
small woodlands, urban parks, and
backyards throughout the state.

FIELD NOTES In winter, the White-breasted often joins
mixed-species foraging groups with the Red-breasted
Nuthatch, *Sitta canadensis* (inset: female, top; male,
bottom). Though similar in behavior, the less
common Red-breasted is noticeably smaller
and has rust-colored underparts, darker on the males.
The Red-breasted forages on small branches and outer twigs.

Year-round | Adult

BROWN CREEPER

Certhia americana L 5.3" (13 cm)

FIELD MARKS
Mottled, streaky brown above

White eyebrow stripe

White underparts

Long, thin decurved bill

Long, graduated tail

Behavior
Camouflaged by streaked brown plumage, climbs upward from the base of a tree, then flies to a lower place on another tree in search of insects and larvae in tree bark. Long, decurved bill helps it to dig prey out of tree bark; its stiff tail feathers serving as a prop against the trunk. Forages by itself in general, unless part of a mixed-species flock in winter. Builds nests behind loose bark of dead or dying trees. Call is a soft, sibilant, almost inaudible *seee*. Song is a high-pitched *seee seeed-see sideeu*, or a similar variation.

Habitat
Found mostly in heavily forested areas. May wander into suburban and urban parks in winter.

Local Sites
These tiny, tree-trunk climbers of the forests are well camouflaged against the bark, so you must look for them carefully. Allegheny National Forest, Erie National Wildlife Refuge, Susquehannock State Forest, and the Pocono Mountains are good places to search.

FIELD NOTES If the creeper suspects the presence of a predator, it will spread its wings and tail, press its body tight against the trunk of a tree, and remain completely motionless. In this pose, its camouflaged plumage makes it almost invisible.

Year-round | Adult

CAROLINA WREN

Thryothorus ludovicianus L 5.5" (14 cm)

FIELD MARKS
Deep rusty brown above with
dark brown bars

Prominent white eye stripe

Warm buff below

White chin and throat

Long, slightly decurved bill

Behavior
Pokes around on ground with its decurved bill, looking
for insects, spiders, snails, fruits, berries, and seeds. A
pair stays together in its territory throughout the year.
Nests in any open cavity of suitable size, including
woodpecker holes, barn rafters, mailboxes, flowerpots,
even boots left outside. From its perch at any time of
day or season, male sings rich, melodious song of
repeated phrases, sometimes starting or ending with a
single note— *chip mediator mediator mediator meep*—
to which female may respond with a low rattle.

Habitat
Found in underbrush of moist woodlands and swamps,
and around human habitation on farms, in wooded
suburbs, and less frequently in city parks.

Local Sites
Well adapted to human activities, these noisy birds are
ubiquitous in rural and suburban areas in the southwestern and southeastern portions of the state.

FIELD NOTES The northern limit of the Carolina Wren's range will
expand and contract in response to the severity of winter
weather. In mild years, it sometimes extends its range into
Canada, but is pushed back by the next harsh winter.

Year-round | Adult

HOUSE WREN

Troglodytes aedon L 4.8" (12 cm)

FIELD MARKS
Grayish or brown upperparts

Fine black barring on wings and tail

Pale gray underparts

Pale faint eye ring, eyebrow

Thin, slightly decurved bill

Behavior
Noisy, conspicuous, and relatively tame, with its tail often cocked upward. Gleans insects and spiders from vegetation. Forages at a variety of levels, including high up in trees. Male begins construction on a number of possible nests in any crevice of suitable size. Female joins him, inspects the nests, and chooses one to complete. Sings exuberantly in a cascade of bubbling, down-slurred trills. Call is a rough *chek-chek,* often running into a chatter.

Habitat
Found in open woodlands and thickets, and in shrubbery around farms, parks, and suburban gardens.

Local Sites
Thickets, woodland edges, shrubby fields, and backyard nesting boxes host summer-breeding pairs throughout the state, especially in rural areas and small towns.

FIELD NOTES The Winter Wren, *Troglodytes troglodytes* (inset), has a short, stubby tail and darker barring on its belly than the House Wren. Its song is a rapid series of melodious trills, and its sharp *chimp-chimp* call is distinctive. The secretive Winter Wren nests in dense brush, especially along stream banks in moist, coniferous woods.

Year-round | Adult male

GOLDEN-CROWNED KINGLET

Regulus satrapa L 4" (10 cm)

FIELD MARKS

Yellow crown patch bordered in black; tuft of orange feathers within yellow on male

Olive green upperparts, pale buff underparts

Broad whitish eyebrow; two whitish wing bars

Behavior

Gleans insects and larvae from bark and leaves, reaching into tiny recesses with its short, straight bill. Also drinks tree sap, sometimes following sapsuckers to fresh drill holes. Constructs a spherical nest of lichen, moss, bark, and feathers. Song is almost inaudibly high, consisting of a series of *tsii* notes becoming louder and chattering toward the end. Call is high, thin *tsii tsii tsii*.

Habitat

Found in dense, coniferous and mixed woodlands.

Local Sites

In the breeding season, look for these birds in conifer woodlands in the mountains above Powdermill Avian Research Center, at World's End and Rickett's Glen State Parks, and along Kittatinny Ridge. Migrants from the north spend winters in woodlands across the state.

FIELD NOTES The closely related Ruby-crowned Kinglet, *Regulus calendula* (inset: male, left; female, right), is rarely seen in the same mixed-species foraging flock in winter as the Golden-crowned, primarily in southeastern Pennsylvania. It is distinguished by its plainer face and its husky *ji-dit* call. The red crown patch of the male Ruby-crowned is exposed only when it is agitated.

Breeding | Adult male

BLUE-GRAY GNATCATCHER

Polioptila caerulea L 4.3" (11 cm)

FIELD MARKS
Male is blue-gray above, female
grayer; both are white below

Long, black tail with white
outer feathers

Black forehead and eyebrow on
male in breeding plumage

Behavior
Often seen near branch tips of deciduous trees,
scouring leaves for small insects, spiders, eggs, and larvae. Sometimes captures prey in flight and may hover
briefly. Male and female together make cup-like nest of
plant fibers, spider webs, moss, and lichens on a branch
or fork of a tree. Emits a querulous *pwee,* intoned like a
question, as well as a high-pitched buzz. Known to
imitate other birds' songs as well, a surprise to birders
expecting this only from mockingbirds and thrashers.

Habitat
Favors moist woodland edges and thickets.

Local Sites
Except in winter, gnatcatchers are common in much of
the state, especially in southern areas. They are easy to
find at Ryerson Station and Yellow Creek State Parks in
the west, and at Marsh Creek State Park and along the
Delaware River in the east.

FIELD NOTES Like many of the smaller songbird species, gnatcatchers are altricial at hatching—naked and unable to see,
requiring complete parental care. Young are fed in the nest for
about two weeks, then outside for an additional period of time.
Avoid disturbing a nest site, as it may sometimes cause the
pair to abandon it and rebuild elsewhere.

Year-round | Adult male

EASTERN BLUEBIRD

Sialia sialis L 7" (18 cm)

FIELD MARKS

Male is bright blue above

Female is a grayer blue above, duller below

Chestnut throat, breast, flanks, and sides of neck

White belly and undertail coverts

Behavior

Hunts from elevated perch in the open, dropping to the ground to seize crickets, grasshoppers, and spiders. Has been observed pouncing on prey it has spotted from as many as 130 feet away. In winter, forms small flocks and roosts communally at night in tree cavities or nest boxes. During courtship, male shows vivid coloring on his side during wing-waving displays beside a chosen nesting site. Nests in woodpecker holes, hollow trees or stumps, and in nest boxes. Call is a musical, rising *too-lee,* extended in song to *too too-lee too-lee.*

Habitat

Found in open woodlands, meadows with scattered trees, farmlands, and orchards.

Local Sites

Their numbers increasing steadily, bluebirds are using bird houses in farmlands statewide, and at many state parks such as Pymatuning, Moraine, and Yellow Creek.

FIELD NOTES The Eastern Bluebird's serious decline in decades past is due largely to competition for nesting sites with two introduced species, the European Starling and the House Sparrow. Specially designed bluebird nesting boxes provided by concerned birders have contributed to a promising comeback.

Year-round | Adult

VEERY

Catharus fuscescens L 7" (18 cm)

FIELD MARKS

Reddish brown above, white below with grayish flanks

Buffy throat and upper breast with light brown spotting

Pale grayish loral area

Brown malar stripe

Behavior

Shy and elusive, forages on the ground and higher up for a variety of insects, caterpillars, spiders, fruit, and berries. If disturbed, flicks wings and raises a small crest. Female builds cup-shaped nest of grass, bark, twigs, and leaves on the ground in underbrush. Calls include an abrupt, descending *veer*, a slow *wee-u*, a harsh chuckle, and a sharp, low *wuck*. Song given at dawn and sunset is a slow, flutelike, somewhat mournful, downward-spiraling *veeerr veeerr veeerr*.

Habitat

Prefers moist woodlands with dense underbrush for nesting. Found in a variety of woodlands, even some suburban backyards, during migration.

Local Sites

Excellent locations for seeking these forest-loving thrushes are the Allegheny National Forest, Susquehannock State Forest, and Beltzville State Park.

FIELD NOTES Veeries generally depart Pennsylvania by the end of September, but ornithologists have not yet determined where exactly they go from there. Previously thought to winter somewhere in northern South America, Veeries have recently been found to spend their winters in central and southern Brazil. While on migration, they are able to fly more than 160 miles in one night at an altitude of over one mile.

Year-round | Adult

WOOD THRUSH

Hylocichla mustelina L 7.8" (20 cm)

FIELD MARKS
Reddish brown above, brightest
on crown and nape

White face and chest streaked
and spotted in black

Rump and tail brownish olive

White eye ring

Behavior
Feeds on the ground or close to it, foraging for insects,
spiders, fruits, and berries. Known to rub ants on its
feathers while preening. During courtship, male chases
female in quick, circling flight. Best known for its loud,
liquid song of three- to five-note phrases, each usually
ending with a trilled whistle, which can be heard in
summer before daybreak or at dusk. Calls include a
rapid *pit-pit-pit* and a rolling *popopopo*.

Habitat
Found in moist, shaded undergrowth of deciduous or
mixed woods, and seldom seen outside of dense forest.

Local Sites
These thrushes favor large, undisturbed woods such as
those in Allegheny National Forest, Bald Eagle State
Park, Susquehannock State Forest, and the Pocono
Mountains, but look for them as well in smaller wood-
lands in just about every state park.

FIELD NOTES The similar, but slightly smaller,
Hermit Thrush, *Catharus guttatus* (inset), breeds
in coniferous forests at high elevations in central
and northeastern Pennsylvania. Look for its olive-
brown back, its reddish brown tail and rump, and
the dark spotting on its breast, as well as its habit of
often flicking its wings and tail.

Year-round | Adults

AMERICAN ROBIN

Turdus migratorius L 10" (25 cm)

FIELD MARKS
Brick red underparts, paler in
female, spotted in juvenile

Brownish gray above with darker
head and tail

White throat and lower belly

Broken white eye ring; yellow bill

Behavior
Best known and largest of the thrushes, often seen on
suburban lawns, hopping about and cocking its head
in search of earthworms. Gleans butterflies, damselflies,
and other flying insects from foliage and sometimes
takes prey in flight. Robins also eat fruit, especially in
fall and winter. This broad plant and animal diet makes
them one of the most successful and wide-ranging
thrushes. Nests in shrubs, trees, and even on sheltered
windowsills. Calls include a low, mellow *pup*, a doubled
or tripled *chok* or *tut*, and a sharp *kli ki ki ki ki*. Song is
a clear, variable *cheerily cheery cheerily cheery*.

Habitat
Common and widespread, forages on lawns and in
woodlands. Winters mostly near thickets, woodland
edges, and urban parks rich in fruit-bearing trees.

Local Sites
Look for the American Robin in your own backyard.
The species is everywhere, including the most crowded
big cities.

FIELD NOTES The juvenile robin, which can be seen every year
between May and September, has a paler breast, like the female
of the species, but its underparts are heavily spotted with brown.
Look as well for the buff fringes on its back and wing feathers
and its short, pale buff eyebrow.

Year-round | Adult

GRAY CATBIRD

Dumetella carolinensis L 8.5" (22 cm)

FIELD MARKS
Dark gray overall

Black cap

Long, black tail, often cocked

Undertail coverts chestnut

Dark eyes; short, dark bill

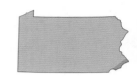

Behavior
Unless singing from an exposed perch, stays low in thick brush, foraging for insects, spiders, berries, and fruit from branches, foliage, and leaf litter. Female builds nest in low shrubs or in small trees with dense growth offering some protection. The catbird got its name from its catlike, downslurred *mew* call. Song intersperses *mew* notes within a variable mixture of melodious, nasal, squeaky, sometimes abrasive but never repeated, notes. Jumps abruptly from one phrase to another in its rambling series of vocalizations.

Habitat
Tends to stay hidden in low, dense thickets of overgrowth in woodlands and residential areas.

Local Sites
A common species, catbirds can be found in thickets in virtually all state and city parks and in semi-rural areas, except heavily wooded forests at high elevations.

FIELD NOTES The Gray Catbird is one of Pennsylvania's few mimics to truly rival the Northern Mockingbird in breadth and variety of imitations. In addition to its catlike *mew*, the catbird can reproduce calls of other birds, of amphibians, even of machinery, and incorporate them into its song.

Year-round | Adult

NORTHERN MOCKINGBIRD

Mimus polyglottos L 10" (25 cm)

FIELD MARKS
Gray overall; darker above

White wing patches and outer
tail feathers flash conspicuously
in flight

Long, blackish wings and tail

Short, black bill

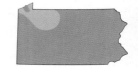

Behavior

The pugnacious Northern Mockingbird will protect its
territory against other birds as well as dogs, cats, and
humans. Has a varied diet that includes berries, grasshoppers, spiders, snails, and earthworms. An expert
mimic, the mockingbird is known for its variety of
songs, learning and imitating calls of many other
species and animals. Typically repeats a song's phrases
three times before beginning a new one. Often sings at
night during nesting season. Call is a loud, sharp *check*.

Habitat

Resides in a variety of habitats, including cities, towns,
and suburbs.

Local Sites

Basically a bird of the southern U.S., this songster is
common in all urban, suburban, and rural areas in the
state's southern counties, except in the high mountains.
Look and listen for it even in the largest cities.

FIELD NOTES The Northern Mockingbird in flight
(inset) reveals conspicuous white patches on its
wings and outer tail feathers. While hunting, it shows
these same white patches in a wing-flashing display
that perhaps serves to startle insects into the open.

Year-round | Adult

BROWN THRASHER

Toxostoma rufum **L** 11.5" (29 cm)

FIELD MARKS
Reddish brown above

Pale buff to white below with
heavy dark streaking

Long, reddish brown tail

Yellow eyes; dark, decurved bill

Two white wing bars

Behavior
Forages through leaf litter for insects, fruit, and grain;
finds additional prey by digging with decurved bill.
Courtship involves little fanfare, the whole process consisting of one or both birds picking up leaves or twigs
and dropping them in front of the other. Nests in
bushes, on ground, or in low trees. Sings from an
exposed perch a long series of varied melodious
phrases, each one given two or three times. Calls
include a loud, smacking *spuck* and a low *churr*.

Habitat
Found in hedgerows, dense brush, and woodland
edges.

Local Sites
Look for these large, loud songsters during breeding
season in brushy fields and woodland edges in every
region of the state except in the highest mountains and
the most heavily populated urban areas.

FIELD NOTES A very creative vocalizer, the Brown Thrasher has
the ability to mimic other birds, but more often sings its own
song—it's got enough of them. It has been reported that the
Brown Thrasher has the largest song repertoire of any North
American bird; more than 1,100 types have been recorded. The
number of songs a male can sing may be an indicator of status
to females seeking a mate.

Nonbreeding | Adult

EUROPEAN STARLING

Sturnus vulgaris L 8.5" (22 cm)

FIELD MARKS

Iridescent black breeding plumage

Buffy tips on back, tail feathers

Fall feathers tipped in white,
giving speckled appearance

Yellow bill in summer; its base is
pale blue on male, pink on female

Behavior

A social and aggressive bird, feeds on a variety of food,
ranging from invertebrates—such as snails, worms, and
spiders—to fruit, berries, grains, seeds, and garbage.
Probes ground, opening bill to create small holes and
expose prey. Usually seen in flocks, except while nesting
in cavities, ranging from crevices in urban settings to
woodpecker holes and nest boxes. Imitates calls of
other species and emits high-pitched notes, including
squeaks, hisses, whistles, rattles, and wheezes.

Habitat

The adaptable starling thrives in a variety of habitats
near humans, including urban centers and farmland.

Local Sites

Big cities, towns, and farmlands are all home to this
ubiquitous import from Europe. Look for immense
flocks that gather during early fall and winter in rural
southeastern areas of the state.

FIELD NOTES A Eurasian species introduced into New York's
Central Park in 1890, the European Starling has since spread
throughout the U.S. and Canada. Abundant, bold, and aggressive, starlings often compete for and take over nest sites of other
native birds, including bluebirds, Wood Ducks, a variety of
woodpeckers, Tree Swallows, and Purple Martins.

Year-round | Adult

CEDAR WAXWING

Bombycilla cedrorum L 7.3" (18 cm)

FIELD MARKS
Distinctive sleek crest

Black mask bordered in white

Brownish head, back, breast, and sides; pale yellow belly; gray rump

Yellow terminal tail band

May have red, waxy tips on wings

Behavior

Eats the most fruit of any North American bird. Up to 84% of its diet are cedar, holly, and hawthorn berries and crabapple fruit. Also eats sap, flower petals, and insects. Moves long distances only when food sources run out. Gregarious in nature, waxwings band together for foraging and protection. Flocks containing several to a few hundred birds may feed side by side in winter, then rapidly disperse, startling potential predators. Call is a high-pitched, trilled *zeeeee.*

Habitat

Found in a variety of open habitats wherever fruit and berries are available.

Local Sites

Inhabiting cities, towns, parks, and gardens, these subtly beautiful birds are present statewide and year-round wherever food is abundant. Look for wandering groups in treetops during the fall, when flock sizes increase.

FIELD NOTES One of the more courteous diners in the bird world, Cedar Waxwings have been known to perch side by side and pass a piece of food down the row, one bird to the next, until one of them decides to eat it. If the bird at the end of the line receives the morsel and is disinclined as well, it is passed right back up the line.

Year-round | Adult male

BLUE-WINGED WARBLER

Vermivora pinus L 4.8" (12 cm)

FIELD MARKS

Male has bright yellow crown and underparts; female duller

Blue-gray wings with two white wing bars

Black eye line

White underside of tail

Behavior

This easily overlooked bird forages low to the ground for insects and spiders. May hover briefly while probing into foliage with long, slender bill. Nests on or near the ground at the base of a shrub or in a clump of grass. Readily hybridizes with Golden-winged Warbler (inset, below). Frequently given call is a gentle *tsip*; also gives a high, slightly buzzy *tzii* in flight. Songs are high-pitched and buzzy: *beeee-bzzzz* or *be-ee-ee-ee-bttttt*.

Habitat

Found in overgrown fields, open brushy woodland edges, and in thickets. Winters in Central America.

Local Sites

This increasing species is generally most common in the state's western and southeastern regions. Moraine and Ryerson State Parks in the west, and Marsh Creek State Park and the Delaware River Valley in the east are all good sites.

FIELD NOTES The Golden-winged Warbler, *Vermivora chrysoptera* (inset: female, top; male, bottom), is declining largely due to hybridization with and displacement by the Blue-winged. The Golden-Winged breeds in central and northeastern Pennsylvania; it shows a yellow forecrown, a striking face pattern, and extensive yellow on the wings. Hybrids show a variety of intermediate characteristics.

Year-round | Adult male

NORTHERN PARULA

Parula americana L 4.8" (11 cm)

FIELD MARKS

Gray-blue above with yellowish green upper back patch

Throat and breast bright yellow with red breast band; white belly

Two white wing bars

Broken white eye ring

Behavior

Pennsylvania's smallest warbler and a very active forager. It can be observed rightside up or upside down on branches, searching for insects, hovering in search of caterpillars or spiders, or in aerial pursuit of flying insects. Prefers to nest in trees covered with Spanish moss or *Usnea* lichen, and if necessary, will fly as far as a mile away to secure a single piece of either plant for use in its nest. Call is a sharp *tsip*. Song can be heard from treetops during nesting or migration; consists of a rising, buzz-like trill, ending in an abrupt *tsip*.

Habitat

Common in mature coniferous or mixed woods.

Local Sites

The southwestern Allegheny Mountains, especially near Powdermill Avian Research Center, and the Delaware Water Gap National Recreation Area offer good chances of seeing these beautiful warblers.

FIELD NOTES The slightly larger Nashville Warbler, *Vermivora ruficapilla* (inset: adult male), is a summer resident, increasing in population in high-elevation portions of central and northeastern Pennsylvania. It is mostly greenish above, mostly yellow below, and has a blue-gray head.

Breeding | Adult male

CHESTNUT-SIDED WARBLER

Dendroica pensylvanica L 5" (13 cm)

FIELD MARKS
Breeding male has yellow
crown; black eye and malar
stripes; chestnut sides

Female has greenish crown
and less chestnut

Two yellowish wing bars;
black-streaked back

Behavior
An active forager, often drooping its wings and cocking
its tail above its back, gleans insects, caterpillars, seeds,
and berries from low foliage or directly from ground.
May sometimes take insects in flight. Nest of grass,
sticks, and roots located near the ground in shrubby
understory.. Call is a loud, sweet *chip*. Male sings conspicuously from exposed perch a whistled *please, please,
pleased to meetcha* or a *wee-weewee-wee-chi-tee-wee*.

Habitat
Breeds in open brushy woodlands, especially second-
growth deciduous ones, and in overgrown fields.
Found in a variety of woodlands during migration.

Local Sites
Look for these birds primarily in shrubby second-
growth woodlands and clearcuts in the northern half of
the state and southward in the Allegheny Mountains.
They are greatest in number during spring migration
in May and fall migration in September.

FIELD NOTES During fall migration, which peaks in
early September, look for fall adults and immatures (inset) that look very different. They are lime
green above and whitish below, with a gray face
and a distinct white eye ring. Adult males retain
dull chestnut sides.

Year-round | Adult male

YELLOW WARBLER

Dendroica petechia L 5" (13 cm)

FIELD MARKS

Bright yellow overall

Plump and short-tailed

Dark eye prominent in yellow face

Male shows distinct reddish streaks below; streaks faint or absent in female

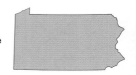

Behavior

Mostly seen alone or in a pair. Forages in trees, shrubs, and bushes, gleaning insects, larvae, and fruit from branches and leaves. Will sometimes spot flying insects from a perch and chase them down. Nests in the forks of trees or bushes at eye level or a little higher. Male and female both feed nestlings. Habitually bobs tail and is quite vocal. Call is a husky, downslurred *tchip* or a thinner *tsip*. Primary song is a rapid, variable *sweet sweet sweet sweeter than sweet.* Alternate songs are longer and more complex.

Habitat

Favors wet habitats, especially near willows and alders; also found in open woodlands, gardens, and orchards.

Local Sites

One of Pennsylvania's most common warblers, it breeds in shrubby fields throughout the state. Hundreds in a day can sometimes be seen during spring and fall migrations at Presque Isle State Park.

FIELD NOTES The misnamed Prairie Warbler, *Dendroica discolor* (inset: male), is actually found mostly in overgrown, shrubby fields with scattered stands of pines, including Christmas tree plantings. Greenish upperparts with faint chestnut marks, yellow underparts, and black streaks on its sides characterize this bird. The male's striking face pattern is also distinctive.

Breeding | Adult male

MAGNOLIA WARBLER

Dendroica magnolia L 5" (13 cm)

FIELD MARKS

Yellow below, heavily streaked in black; blue-gray above with blackish and olive patches

White subterminal band on tail

Breeding male has broad black eye line and white eyebrow

Behavior

Forages alone or in a pair, gleaning insects, larvae, caterpillars, and spiders from branches and leaves. Fans its tail frequently, revealing black-and-white tail pattern. Nests close to the ground in a conifer. Calls include a high-pitched *enk*, given often in fall migration, and a high, buzzy *zee*, given in flight. Males sings from conspicuous perch a variable, short, musical *weeta weeta wit-chew* or an unaccented *sing sweet*.

Habitat

Breeds in cool, damp coniferous and mixed woods at high elevations. Especially associated with hemlocks.

Local Sites

Look for the Magnolia Warbler in the Allegheny National Forest, on mountaintops above Powdermill Avian Research Center, and in the Delaware Water Gap National Recreation Area.

FIELD NOTES The Yellow-rumped Warbler, *Dendroica coronata* (inset: breeding male), is abundant in migration across Pennsylvania and locally common at other times of year. Breeding birds of the northeastern mountains show blue-gray upperparts and yellow side and crown patches. Wintering birds at Presque Isle and in the southeastern counties are much drabber and browner overall.

Year-round | Adult male

BLACK-THROATED BLUE WARBLER

Dendroica caerulescens L 5.3" (13 cm)

FIELD MARKS

Male is dark blue above, white below, with black face, throat, and sides

Female is brownish above, buffy below, with pale eyebrow

White patch at base of primaries is smaller on female

Behavior

Seen alone or in a pair, which is the easiest way to identify the female. Forages fairly low in trees and over-growth for insects and larvae. May also feed on fruit and tree sap during migration. Builds nest with various plant materials in the fork of a low shrub or sapling. Calls include a popping *tuk* and a prolonged *tseet* in flight. Primary song is a slow series of buzzy notes, rising at the end: *zhee zhee zhee zeeee.*

Habitat

Breeds in high-elevation hardwood forests with thick shrubby underbrush. Found in a variety of woods and shrubby areas in migration. Males and females winter separately on a number of Caribbean islands.

Local Sites

Allegheny National Forest, World's End State Park, and Delaware Water Gap National Recreation Area.

FIELD NOTES The Cerulean Warbler, *Dendroica cerulea* (inset: male), is another largely blue wood-warbler in Pennsylvania. The male is sky blue above and white below, with black streaking on his sides and breast. The female is bluish gray above with a buffy breast and throat and a whitish eyebrow. This species nests high in deciduous trees, and tends to stay high, making it quite a challenge to spot one.

Year-round | Adult male

BLACK-THROATED GREEN WARBLER

Dendroica virens L 5" (13 cm)

FIELD MARKS

Yellow face with greenish ear patch; greenish upperparts

Blackish wings with two white wing bars; whitish below

Male has black throat, upper breast, and streaks on its flanks; female has less black

Behavior

Tends to forage away from the tips of branches at about mid-level, gleaning insects, caterpillars, and larvae, and some berries while in migration. Builds nest of grasses, plants, and stems in fork of a deciduous tree or, less frequently, a conifer. Calls are a soft, flat *tsip* and a high, sweet *see*. Song given near nest to attract mate is a variable, whistled, buzzy *zee-zee-zee-zoo-zee*. Song given at edge of territory to ward off other males is a more deliberate *zoo zee zoo zoo zee*.

Habitat

Breeds primarily in hardwood forests, but sometimes also in mixed woods. Found in a variety of wooded and brushy areas during migration.

Local Sites

Allegheny National Forest, Susquehannock State Forest, Bald Eagle State Park, and the Pocono Mountains are among this warbler's strongholds in Pennsylvania.

FIELD NOTES Wood-warblers number about 116 species, 57 in North America, over 30 of which frequent the Appalachians. North American wood-warblers have undergone significant recent declines, resulting chiefly from habitat destruction. Since most species migrate to the tropics they are at risk there and along their migration route as well. Many species' winter ranges are smaller than their breeding ranges, which amplifies the danger.

Breeding | Adult male

BLACKBURNIAN WARBLER

Dendroica fusca L 5" (13 cm)

FIELD MARKS

Male has distinctive orange and black facial pattern; black above with extensive white patches

Female and fall male: paler yellow on throat

White belly and undertail coverts; sides streaked with black

Behavior

Tends to remain at the treetops, gleaning insects, caterpillars, and berries from foliage and twigs. Solitary and territorial during nesting period, but will forage with other species such as chickadees, kinglets, and nut-hatches after nestlings fledge. Calls include a rich *tsip* and a buzzy *zzee* in flight. Primary song is a high-pitched, ascending series of notes, ending with an almost inaudible trill: *see-see-see-see-ti-ti-ti-siiii.*

Habitat

Stays mostly in the upper branches of coniferous and mixed forests while breeding. Found in a variety of woodlands and woodland edges during migration.

Local Sites

Allegheny National Forest, Susquehannock State Forest, World's End State Park, and Delaware Water Gap National Recreation Area all host good numbers of nesting Blackburnians between April and August.

FIELD NOTES Like other juvenile warblers, young Blackburnians will follow their parents while they forage and beg for food with noisy *chip* notes. Immatures show a dark ear patch outlined in drab yellow and a greenish forehead with a distinctive patch of pale yellow. Look also for the yellowish streaks on their backs.

Breeding | Adult male

BLACK-AND-WHITE WARBLER

Mniotilta varia L 5.5" (13 cm)

FIELD MARK

Boldly striped black-and-white on head, body, and undertail coverts

Male's throat and cheeks are black; in winter, chin is white

Females and immatures have white cheeks and throats

Behavior

Creeps around branches and up and down tree trunks, foraging like a nuthatch or creeper. Probes crevices in bark of trees with its long bill for insects, caterpillars, and spiders. Nests on the ground or in the hollow of a stump or log. If disturbed at nest, female drags wings on the ground with tail spread for distraction. Primary song is a variable, long, rhythmic *weesee weesee weesee weesee*; calls include a dull *chip* and a *seet-seet* in flight.

Habitat

Found in woodlands, both deciduous and mixed, as well as forested margins of swamps and rivers.

Local Sites

Find them in spring and summer in Allegheny National Forest, the hills around Powdermill Avian Research Center, and Bald Eagle and Ricketts Glen State Parks.

FIELD NOTES The only other warbler with a foraging style like the Black-and-white's is the Yellow-throated Warbler, *Dendroica dominica* (inset). In summer, it inhabits many of the same mature woods as the Black-and-white in southwestern and southeastern Pennsylvania, but tends to forage higher. Look for its bright yellow chin and throat, its black face, and its white eyebrow.

Year-round | Adult male

AMERICAN REDSTART

Setophaga ruticilla L 5.3" (13 cm)

FIELD MARKS
Male is glossy black above and
on hood; bright orange patches
on sides, wings, and tail

Female gray-olive above; orange
patches replaced with yellow

White belly and undertail coverts

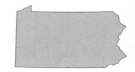

Behavior
Often fans tail and spreads wings when perched. Darts
suddenly to snare flying insects. Also takes insects,
caterpillars, spiders, berries, fruit, and seeds from
branches and foliage. Nests in forks of trees or bushes
generally 10 to 20 feet from the ground. Song is a highly variable series of high, thin notes usually followed by
a single, wheezy, downslurred note: *zee zee zee zee
zweeah.* Calls include a thin, squeaky *chip* and a clear,
penetrating *seep* in flight.

Habitat
Found in moist deciduous and mixed woodlands with
thick undergrowth; also in wooded riparian zones and
second-growth woodlands.

Local Sites
Common in woodlands throughout the state, especially
in Allegheny National Forest, Ricketts Glen State Park,
and Delaware Water Gap National Recreation Area.

FIELD NOTES The female American Redstart
(inset) shows yellow patches wherever the
male shows orange, except in some older females
who have acquired an orange cast to their plumage.
Females are further set apart by a light gray head
and an olive-green back. Immature males resemble
females, but with some black spotting on their lores and breast.

Year-round | Adult

OVENBIRD

Seiurus aurocapilla L 6" (15 cm)

FIELD MARKS

Russet crown bordered in black

Olive-brown above, white below
with dark brown streaks

Brown malar stripe, white chin

Bold white eye ring

Pinkish bill and legs

Behavior

Typically seen on the ground; walks rather than hops;
tail cocked, wings dropped, and head bobbing. Forages
among leaves and twigs for insects, caterpillars, earthworms, snails, seeds, fruit, and berries. Known to kick
up leaf litter to expose prey, a strategy more commonly
employed by sparrows than warblers. Nests on the
ground in small depression covered with grasses and
leaves and entered on the side, resembling a tiny dutch
oven (pictured, opposite). Primary song is a loud,
ascending *TEA-cher TEA-cher TEA-cher*. Calls include a
loud, sharp *tsick*, given rapidly if alarmed, and a high,
thin *seee* in flight. Also gives an elaborate flight song.

Habitat

Found in mature hardwood, deciduous, and mixed
forests, where it stays primarily in thick undergrowth.

Local Sites

The loud song of the Ovenbird can be heard in every
forest in the state. Listen for it in Allegheny National
Forest, Bald Eagle State Park, and Beltzville State Park.

FIELD NOTES Ovenbirds are often easier to hear than to see, as
the song of one male will invariably elicit a response from a
neighboring male, producing a domino effect until the woods
resonate with their competing melodies.

Year-round | Adult

LOUISIANA WATERTHRUSH

Seiurus motacilla L 6" (15 cm)

FIELD MARKS

Olive-brown above and on crown

Eyebrow is pale buff in front of eye, whiter and broader behind

White underparts with dark streaking; salmon-buff flanks

White, unstreaked chin and throat

Behavior

Bobs its tail sideways, slowly but constantly, as it forages on the ground, walking rather than hopping. Feeds on aquatic and terrestrial insects, mollusks, and small fish along stream banks or in shallows. Nests under roots or in crevices in riparian areas. Sings a loud, musical song which begins with three to five clear, downslurred notes, followed by a brief, rapid jumble: *seeeu seeeu seeeu seewit seewit ch-wit it-chu*. Calls include a loud, rich *chik* and a high *zeet* in flight.

Habitat

The Louisianna Waterthrush is found near streams in dense woodlands; also in wooded floodplains and rarely in swamps. Highly intolerant of polluted waters.

Local Sites

This warbler is common in spring and summer in most of the state, especially at Powdermill Avian Research Center, Ryerson Station and Ohiopyle State Parks, and Delaware Water Gap National Recreation Area.

FIELD NOTES The Louisiana Waterthrush and its very similarly plumaged cousin, the Northern Waterthrush, *Seiurus noveboracensis*, both forage on the ground in wet habitats for similar prey. They can be differentiated by the Northern's lightly streaked throat, bolder streaking on its underparts, and its shorter, thinner bill. Northern is typically found at ponds and swamps.

Year-round | Adult male

COMMON YELLOWTHROAT

Geothlypis trichas L 5" (13 cm)

FIELD MARKS
Adult male shows broad, black mask bordered above by light gray

Female lacks black mask, has whitish patch around eyes

Grayish olive upperparts; bright yellow throat and breast; pale yellow undertail coverts

Behavior
Generally remains close to the ground, skulking and hiding in undergrowth. May also be seen climbing vertically on stems and singing from exposed perches. While foraging, cocks tail and hops on ground to glean insects, caterpillars, and spiders from foliage, twigs, and reeds. Nests atop piles of weeds and grass, or in small shrubs. One version of variable song is a loud, rolling *wichity wichity wichity wichity wich*. Calls include a husky *tshep*, a rapid chatter, and a buzzy *dzip* in flight.

Habitat
Stays low in marshes, shrubby fields, woodland edges, and thickets near water.

Local Sites
Abundant at virtually all lakes, ponds, and fields in the state, these warblers are easy to find at Moraine, Yellow Creek, and Marsh Creek State Parks.

FIELD NOTES The largest North American warbler at 7.5", the Yellow-breasted Chat, *Icteria virens* (inset: male), is also an elusive skulker. Like the Yellowthroat, it remains low to the ground, hidden in dense vegetation. Listen for its harsh, jumbled, unmusical song, given from a perch or in flight.

Year-round | Adult male

HOODED WARBLER

Wilsonia citrina L 5.3" (13 cm)

FIELD MARKS

Bright yellow face bordered by black hood on male

Female shows variable amount of black around yellow face

Olive-green above, yellow below with white undertail

Behavior

Constantly opens and closes its tail feathers, revealing white spots on the corners of its tail, as it forages low in trees and shrubs or on the ground for insects, caterpillars, and spiders. Female builds nest of leaves, plant material, spider's silk, and fur; nest located low in shrubs or small trees. Male sings persistently, but often from a concealed perch, a clear, whistled *ta-wee ta-wee ta-wee ta-wee tee-too*, with an emphatic ending. Call given by both sexes is a loud *chink*.

Habitat

Tends to remain close to the ground, often hidden, in thick understory of mature deciduous forests.

Local Sites

The western third of Pennsylvania is this species' stronghold. Moraine, Yellow Creek, Ryerson, and Ohiopyle State Parks are all good places to look in spring and summer.

FIELD NOTES The Kentucky Warbler, *Oporornis formosus* (inset: male), like the Hooded, has bright yellow underparts and olive-green upperparts, but is distinguished by yellow spectacles separating the black on its crown from the black on its face and neck. Both species largely remain hidden in overgrowth, so listen for the Kentucky's low *chup* call and for its song, a rolling, repeated *churree*.

Breeding | 1st spring male

SCARLET TANAGER

Piranga olivacea L 7" (18 cm)

FIELD MARKS
Breeding male has bright red
body and black wings and tail; 1st
spring male has browner wings

Female is olive above with darker
wings and tail, and yellow below

Fall adult male resembles female

Behavior
Forages for insects, berries, and fruit mostly high in the
tops of trees, but will also take food from the ground or
snag insects on the fly. Courtship display consists of
male perching below prospective mate and spreading
his wings to reveal his scarlet back. Male's song is
robinlike but raspier, given to defend territory and
attract a mate: *querit queer querry querit queer*. Female
sings a similar song, but softer and shorter. Call is a
hoarse *chip* or *chip-burr*.

Habitat
This resident of the forest interior is found in almost
any mature woodland that is not heavily fragmented.

Local Sites
Woodlands across the state are home to this beautiful
treetop songster. Look for it in Allegheny National Forest, as well as Ryerson Station, Yellow Creek,
Bald Eagle, and Ricketts Glen State Parks.

FIELD NOTES The female Scarlet Tanager (inset) is easily
set apart from the breeding male by olive upperparts
and yellow underparts, but the male molts into a similar
plumage after breeding. Note his still darker wings and
tail though. In late summer, you may even find a male in
mid-molt with green, yellow, and red splotches.

Year-round | Adult female

EASTERN TOWHEE

Pipilo erythrophthalmus L 7.5" (19 cm)

FIELD MARKS
Male has black hood, upperparts
Female similarly patterned, but
black areas replaced by brown
Rufous sides; white underparts
White corners on long tail
Juvenile streaked light brown

Behavior
Stays low to the ground, scratching leaf litter frequently
with feet together, head held low, and tail up, exposing
prey such as seeds and insects. Also forages for grasshoppers, spiders, moths, and fruit. Male fans his wings
and tail during courtship, displaying contrasting white
patches on his primaries and tertials. Nests on the
ground, near shrubs. Sings from an exposed perch a
loud, ringing *drink your tea*, sometimes shortened to
drink tea. Also calls in an emphatic, upslurred *chewink*.

Habitat
Prefers second-growth woodlands with dense shrubs,
brushy thickets, and extensive leaf litter. Also found in
brambly fields, suburban hedgerows, riparian areas,
and forest clearings.

Local Sites
Common in virtually all forests and small woodlands,
the towhee's call is heard abundantly at Ohiopyle,
Yellow Creek, Bald Eagle, and Marsh Creek State Parks.

FIELD NOTES The juvenile Eastern Towhee has a brown cap,
wings, and tail, and is heavily streaked with brown, which is
especially distinct on its buff underparts. Look for one trailing
its parents only between May and August; the molt into full adult
plumage takes place during its first fall.

Breeding | Adult

CHIPPING SPARROW

Spizella passerina L 5.5" (14 cm)

FIELD MARKS

Breeding adult shows bright chestnut crown, white eyebrow, gray cheek and nape

Winter adult has streaked brown crown and a brown face

Streaked brown wings and back, unstreaked gray breast and belly

Behavior

Forages on the ground for insects, caterpillars, spiders, and seeds. May be found foraging in small family flocks in late summer. Along with the related Field Sparrow (p. 229) and American Tree Sparrow (inset, below), known to employ the clever strategy of landing atop a reed so as to bend it by the force of its weight and more easily extract seeds from the reed tip. Nests close to the ground in branches or vine tangles. Sings from a high perch a one-pitched, rapid-fire trill of dry *chip* notes. Call in flight is a sharp *tseet*, otherwise a high *tsip*.

Habitat

Found in suburban parks and gardens, woodland edges and clearings; prefers conifers when breeding.

Local Sites

Abundant in cities, towns, and woodlands, these sparrows can be seen in spring and summer at Moraine, Yellow Creek, World's End, and Beltzville State Parks; or in many backyards.

FIELD NOTES Once Chipping Sparrows head farther south in October, they are replaced in brushy fields and woodland edges by American Tree Sparrows, *Spizella arborea* (inset: nonbreeding),characterized by a head striped with rufous and gray and a dark central breast splotch. Listen for its sharp, high, bell-like *tink* notes.

Year-round | Adult

FIELD SPARROW

Spizella pusilla L 5.5" (15 cm)

FIELD MARKS
Gray face with rufous crown;
some with rufous behind eyes

Distinct white eye ring; pink bill

Streaked brown back and wings

Breast and sides gray or buff-
colored; belly grayish white

Behavior
Remains low to the ground in fields and open brush,
foraging for insects, caterpillars, seeds, and spiders. Will
land atop a reed or grass stem in order to bend it down to
the ground with its weight and more easily extract seeds.
Found singly or in a pair in spring and summer; forms
small family groups after breeding; and in larger, mixed-
species foraging flocks in winter. Female builds nest of
grasses, leaves, and roots on the ground or in a bush
low to the ground, often near water. Song is a series of
clear, plaintive whistles accelerating into a trill. Call
note is a high, sharp *chip*. In flight, listen for the Field
Sparrow's high, loud *tseees*.

Habitat
Found in open, brushy woodlands; shrubby, overgrown
fields; and in wooded clearings near water.

Local Sites
Scrubby fields around Shenango Reservoir, Yellow
Creek State Park, and Middle Creek Wildlife Manage-
ment Area are fine spots to see this common nester.

FIELD NOTES Field Sparrows flourished with the widespread
abandonment of farmlands in the early 1900s, which opened up
countless acres of ideal nesting habitat. Now that suburbs and
successional forests are taking over farmlots across the eastern
seaboard, their numbers are declining.

Year-round | Adult

SAVANNAH SPARROW

Passerculus sandwichensis L 5.5" (14 cm)

FIELD MARKS

Yellow or whitish eyebrow

Pale median crown stripe on streaked crown

Dark brown streaked upperparts

White below with brown streaking on chin, breast, and flanks

Behavior

Forages on the ground singly or in a pair for insects, spiders, and seeds in spring and summer. Forms loose flocks in migration and winter that feed primarily on seeds and berries. Sometimes scratches in dirt like a towhee. Nests on the ground in small depression concealed by grasses. Song begins with two or three *chip* notes, followed by long buzzy trill and a final *tip* note. Common call is a high *tip*. Flight call is a thin, descending *tseew*.

Habitat

Found in a variety of open habitats, such as grasslands, farm fields, and pastures.

Local Sites

Piney Tract, Pymatuning State Park, and farmlands east of the lower Susquehanna River are home to these sparrows in spring and summer.

FIELD NOTES The larger Fox Sparrow, *Passerella iliaca* (inset), appears throughout Pennsylvania in migration and in the southwestern and southeastern portions of the state in winter. Like the Savannah, it remains close to the ground, sometimes foraging like a towhee, but it prefers more densely wooded areas. It is much more rufous overall, and its breast streaking converges into a large central splotch.

Year-round | Adult

SONG SPARROW

Melospiza melodia L 6.3" (16 cm)

FIELD MARKS
Underparts whitish, with streaks on sides and breast that converge into a dark breast spot

Streaked brown and gray above; broad, grayish eyebrow; broad, dark malar stripe

Long, rounded tail

Behavior
Forages in trees and bushes and on ground for insects, larvae, seeds, and berries, sometimes scratching ground to unearth food. Nests on the ground or near it in trees and bushes. Female broods young while male defends territory intently, singing from exposed perch and battling competitors. Perches in the open, belting out its melodious song, three to four short, clear notes followed by a buzzy *tow-wee*, then a trill. Common call is a nasal, hollow *chimp*. Flight call is a clear, rising *seeet*.

Habitat
Common in suburban and rural gardens, weedy fields, dense streamside thickets, and forest edges.

Local Sites
Find the Song Sparrow in suburban backyards or local parks year-round anywhere in the state.

FIELD NOTES The Swamp Sparrow, *Melospiza georgiana* (inset: breeding), tends to remain in wetter areas than the Song Sparrow. It breeds throughout the state and is a year-round resident around the lower Susquehanna and Delaware Rivers. Look for its rufous and gray crown, its reddish brown wings, and the blurry streaks on its grayish breast.

Year-round | Adult

WHITE-THROATED SPARROW

Zonotrichia albicollis L 6.8" (17 cm)

FIELD MARKS

Broad eyebrow is yellow in front of eye, white or tan behind

Black lateral crown stripes and eye lines; white throat bordered by gray

Streaked rusty brown above, grayish below

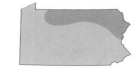

Behavior

Employs double-scratch foraging method, raking leaf litter with backward kick of both feet, keeping head held low and tail pointed up. Also forages in bushes and trees for seeds, tree buds, and insects. Nests close to or on ground, often at forest edges near water. Calls include a sharp *pink* and a drawn out, lisping *tseep*, given in flight. Its song, given year-round, is a thin whistle of one or two single notes then three or four longer notes: *pure sweet Canada Canada Canada.*

Habitat

Winters in woodland undergrowth, brush, and gardens. Breeds primarily in shrubby wetlands.

Local Sites

These birds breed in widely scattered areas of the Susquehannock State Forest, World's End State Park, and the Pocono Mountains. Commonly seen at backyard feeders in winter.

FIELD NOTES A migrant and winter visitor to Pennsylvania is the White-crowned Sparrow, *Zonotrichia leucophrys* (inset). With similar habitat and behavioral characteristics as the White-throated, the White-crowned is distinguished by its lack of yellow in front of the eye and its grayish throat, not as clearly marked off from its breast.

Year-round | Adult male "Slate-colored"

DARK-EYED JUNCO

Junco hyemalis L 6.3" (16 cm)

FIELD MARKS

Dark gray hood and upperparts on male, brownish on female

White outer tail feathers in flight

White belly and undertail coverts

Pale pinkish bill

Juvenile streaked brown overall

Behavior
Forages by scratching on ground to expose food and by gleaning seeds, grain, berries, insects, caterpillars, and fruit from vegetation. Occasionally gives chase to a flying insect. Forms flocks in winter, when males may stay farther north or at greater elevations than immatures and females. Nests on or close to ground, sheltered by a bush or in a cavity such as a tree root. Song, given year-round, is a short, musical trill on one pitch. Calls include a sharp *dit,* and a rapid twittering in flight.

Habitat
Winters in a wide variety of habitats, especially patchy wooded areas and including backyard feeding stations. Breeds in high-elevation mixed woodlands.

Local Sites
Look for juncos nesting in the Allegheny National Forest, World's End and Ricketts Glen State Parks, and the Pocono Mountains. In winter, a backyard bird feeder is almost sure to have a flock all season long.

FIELD NOTES Though widely scattered geographically and fairly different in their field marks, 12 subspecies of Dark-eyed Junco are recognized by the American Ornithologists' Union. A western form, the "Oregon" junco, is an accidental vagrant rarely seen at feeding stations in Pennsylvania in winter. It shows a black or dark hood, a reddish brown back, a gray rump, and a white belly.

Year-round | Adult male

NORTHERN CARDINAL

Cardinalis cardinalis L 8.8" (22 cm)

FIELD MARKS

Male is red overall; black on face

Female is buffy brown tinged with red on wings, crest, and tail

Large, conspicuous crest

Cone-shaped, reddish bill; blackish on juvenile

Behavior
Generally seen alone or in a pair in summer; in small groups in winter. Forages on the ground or low in shrubs for insects, seeds, leaf buds, berries, and fruit. Territorially aggressive, attacks not only other birds, but also itself, reflected in windows, rear-view mirrors, and chrome surfaces. Nests in forks of trees and bushes, or in tangles of twigs and vines. Call is a sharp, somewhat metallic *chip*. Sings a variety of melodious songs year-round, including a *cue cue cue*, a *cheer cheer cheer,* and a *purty purty purty*. Listen for courtship duets in spring.

Habitat
Found in gardens and parks, woodland edges, stream-side thickets, and practically any environment that provides thick, brushy cover. The cardinal has adapted so well to landscaped yards and backyard feeders that it continues to expand its range northward into Canada.

Local Sites
These birds are a year-round delight in backyards, parks, and every other habitat throughout the state except the highest mountaintops.

FIELD NOTES Cardinals may appear sleek and streamlined in summer and plumper in winter. This is because, as with many birds, they fluff out their body feathers in colder months in order to create pockets of air that conserve body heat.

Breeding | Adult male

ROSE-BREASTED GROSBEAK

Pheucticus ludovicianus L 8" (20 cm)

FIELD MARKS
Breeding male has black hood
and upperparts, rose red
breast and wing linings, and
white underparts

Female brownish above with
white eyebrow and whitish,
streaked underparts

Behavior
Forages in trees and shrubs for insects, caterpillars,
seeds, fruit, and berries. Occassionally hovers to pick
food off tips of branches. Forms flocks in migration
and winter. Courtship display consists of male and
female rubbing bills. Nests in vines, shrubs, or low in
trees. Male sings almost constantly a robinlike series of
warbled phrases. Call is a sharp *eek*.

Habitat
Prefers second-growth deciduous woodlands, but also
found in wooded swamps and some suburban parks.

Local Sites
Near the southernmost limit of their continental range,
Pennsylvania's populations of Rose-breasteds are most
commonly found in the Allegheny National Forest,
Susquehannock State Forest, hills around Powdermill
Avian Research Center, and in the Pocono Mountains.

FIELD NOTES The female Rose-breasted (inset), with its brownish
streaked plumage, is easily distinguished from the adult male,
but it can be difficult to tell apart from an
immature male. The first-fall male is also
brownish and streaked above, but has a
buffier breast than the female and may show
some pink. An immature male will also sing,
unlike the female.

Breeding | Adult male

INDIGO BUNTING

Passerina cyanea L 5.5" (14 cm)

FIELD MARKS
Breeding male deep blue overall, darker on head; blackish wings

Female is brownish, with diffuse streaking on breast and flanks and a bluish tail

Fall male has varied amount of brown on back, breast, and lores

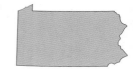

Behavior
Forages for insects and larvae from ground level to canopy in spring and summer, switching to a seed and berry diet in the fall. Uses heavy conical bill to crack or hull seeds. Forms mixed-species flocks in migration and winter. Nests in shrubs or low in trees, using weeds, bark, grass, and leaves. Territorially aggressive males will often chase away other males. Call is a dry, metallic *pik*. Sings from high perch a series of varied phrases, usually doubled. Second-year males appear to learn songs from competing males, not from parents.

Habitat
Prefers forest edges and bushy transition zones between fields or clearcuts and second-growth woodlands.

Local Sites
Found commonly statewide in spring and summer, male Indigos sing from high treetops in the Shenango Reservoir area, and Yellow Creek, Ryerson Station, and Marsh Creek State Parks.

FIELD NOTES The female Indigo Bunting (inset), with her brown back, buffy wing bars, and slightly streaked undersides tends to resemble a sparrow if seen alone. Look for her bluish tail, bicolored bill, and unstreaked head and back to tell her apart.

Breeding | Adult male

BOBOLINK

Dolichonyx oryzivorus L 7" (18 cm)

FIELD MARKS
Breeding male is mostly black with yellowish hindneck and white scapulars and rump

Female is buffy overall with dark streaks on head, back, and sides

Fall birds resemble female except show rich yellow-buff below

Behavior
Typically feeds during the day on insects, caterpillars, grasses, seeds, and grains. Has been observed feeding at night in agricultural fields while in migration. Flocks may number in the thousands in migration. Nests on the ground in tall grasses or weeds. Male arrives first on breeding grounds to stake out territory and engage in flight displays while singing his loud, bubbling, eponymous song *bob-o-link bob-o-link blink blank blink.* Call is a loud, sharp *pink.*

Habitat
Found in hayfields, weedy meadows, and open grasslands. Winters as far south as Argentina.

Local Sites
Pymatuning State Park, the Piney Tract, and Middle Creek Wildlife Management Area host large breeding populations of these birds. Look for them in spring when the males sing their bubbly song in courtship flights over grasslands.

FIELD NOTES The female Bobolink (inset) and fall male show streaking similar to a sparrow's, but are in general a warmer buff below. Some males do not actually molt into this plumage until they are in the middle of migration. Note as well the Bobolink's sharply pointed tail feathers.

Year-round | Adult male

RED-WINGED BLACKBIRD

Agelaius phoeniceus L 8.8" (22 cm)

FIELD MARKS

Male is glossy black with bright red shoulder patches broadly edged in buffy yellow

Females densely streaked overall

Pointed black bill

Wings slightly rounded at tips

Behavior

Runs and hops while foraging for insects, seeds, and grains in pastures and open fields. Male reveals red shoulder patches when he sings from a perch, often atop a cattail or tall weed stalk. Territorially aggressive, a male's social status is dependent on the amount of red he displays. Nests colonially in cattails, bushes, or dense grass near water. Song is a hoarse, gurgling *konk-la-reee*, ending in a trill. Call is a low *chuk* note.

Habitat

Breeds mainly in freshwater marshes and wet fields with thick vegetation. During winter, flocks forage in wooded swamps and farm fields.

Local Sites

Look for the Red-winged in summer at Geneva Marsh, Yellow Creek State Park, and Middle Creek Wildlife Management Area. Immense flocks of tens of thousands gather in fall and winter at farmlands near the lower Susquehanna River.

FIELD NOTES Usually less visible within large flocks of singing males, the female Red-winged (inset) is streaked dark brown above and has dusky white underparts heavily streaked with dark brown. In winter you may find a whole flock of just females.

Breeding | Adult

EASTERN MEADOWLARK

Sturnella magna L 9.5" (24 cm)

FIELD MARKS

Yellow below, with black V-shaped breast band, obscured in winter

Black-and-whitish striped crown with yellow supraloral area

Brown above, streaked with black

White outer tail feathers

Behavior

Flicks tail open and shut while foraging on the ground. Feeds mainly on insects during spring and summer, seeds and grain in fall and winter. Forms small flocks in fall and winter. Female constructs a domed nest on the ground, often woven into the surrounding live grasses. Male known to brood while female starts second nest. Often perches on fence posts or telephone poles to sing three to five (and sometimes more) loud, descending whistles: *tsweee-tsweee-TSWEEEOOO*. Calls include a buzzy *dzert*, a high-pitched chatter, and a whistled *weeet* in flight.

Habitat

Prefers the open space offered by grasslands, pastures, meadows, farm fields, and large lawns.

Local Sites

Pymatuning State Park, the Piney Tract, fields near Yellow Creek State Park, and farm fields near the lower Susquehanna River have large breeding populations of meadowlarks in spring and summer.

FIELD NOTES Though its breeding range has been advancing northward due to the widespread clearing of forests, the Eastern Meadowlark population has been slowly declining in the eastern states during the past few decades as it loses suitable habitat to suburban sprawl.

Year-round | Adult male "Purple"

COMMON GRACKLE

Quiscalus quiscula L 12.5" (32 cm)

FIELD MARKS

Plumage appears all black; in good light, male shows glossy purplish blue hood

Female plumage not as iridescent

Long, wedge-shaped tail

Pale yellow eyes

Behavior

Usually seen in a flock, foraging on the ground for insects, spiders, grubs, and earthworms. Also wades into shallow water to forage for minnows and crayfish, and will feed on eggs and baby birds. In winter, moves to large, noisy, communal roosts in the evening. Courtship consists of male puffing out shoulder feathers, drooping his wings, and singing. Both sexes sing a mechanical, squeaky *readle-eak*. Call is a loud *chuck*.

Habitat

Found in farm fields, pastures, marshes, and around human habitation. Requires open wooded areas, particularly those with conifers, for nesting and roosting.

Local Sites

Abundant breeders in cities, suburbs, and parks throughout the state, the aggressive grackles gather by the tens of thousands in fall and winter at farmlands near the lower Susquehanna River.

FIELD NOTES Two distinct subspecies of Common Grackle are found in Pennsylvania. To the west of the Appalachians, look for the "Bronzed Grackle," *Q. q. versicolor*, characterized by an iridescent bronze back and purple tail. On the other side of the mountains, look for the "Purple Grackle," *Q. q. stonei* (pictured, opposite), which shows iridescent bands of blue, green, bronze, and purple on its back and wings coverts.

Year-round | Adult male

BROWN-HEADED COWBIRD

Molothrus ater L 7.5" (19 cm)

FIELD MARKS

Male's brown head contrasts with metallic black body

Female gray-brown above, paler below with a whitish throat

Short, dark, pointed bill

Juvenile streaked below

Behavior

Often forages on the ground among herds of cattle, feeding on insects flushed by the grazing animals. Also feeds heavily on seeds and grain. Generally cocks its tail up while feeding. A nest parasite, it will wander for many miles to lay its eggs in the nests of other species, leaving the responsibilities of feeding and fledging of young to the host birds. Primary song is a series of liquid, purring gurgles followed by a high whistle: *bub ko lum tseeee.* Call is a soft *kek.* Females also give a dry chatter, while males emit a modulated whistle in flight.

Habitat

Found in open areas such as farmlands, pastures, forest edges, and lawns. Also seen around human habitation.

Local Sites

These birds breed throughout the state in virtually every city, town, field, and farm. Large flocks spend the winter with blackbirds and grackles at farmlands east of the lower Susquehanna River.

FIELD NOTES The Brown-headed Cowbird flourishes in most of North America, adapting to newly cleared lands and exposing new songbirds—now more than 200 species—to its parasitic brooding habit. The female Brown-headed Cowbird lays up to 40 eggs a season in the nests of host birds, leaving the task of raising her young to the host species.

Year-round | Adult male

BALTIMORE ORIOLE

Icterus galbula L 8.3" (21 cm)

FIELD MARKS

Male has black hood and back; bright orange rump and underparts; large orange patches on tail

Female is olive-brown above, orange below, with some black on head and throat

Black wings with white edging

Behavior

Mainly eats caterpillars, but will feed as well on other insects, berries, fruit, even flower nectar. Forages high in bushes and trees. Male bows to female, with wings and tail spread, during courtship. Suspends its bag-shaped nest near the tip of a tree branch about 30 feet up, an adaptation designed to deter egg-eating snakes and mammals. Calls include a whistled *hew-li* and a dry chatter. Song is a variable series of sweet, musical whistles.

Habitat

Breeds in deciduous woodlands and wooded suburbs. In migration, found wherever there are tall trees.

Local Sites

Greatly increasing as breeders in suburban yards and parks throughout the state, these orioles are conspicuous treetop singers at Moraine, Yellow Creek, and Marsh Creek State Parks. During spring and fall migration, hundreds often gather at Presque Isle State Park.

FIELD NOTES Sharing much of the same breeding grounds as the Baltimore Oriole, the Orchard Oriole, *Icterus spurius*, spends most of its time in open woodlands, farmlands, and orchards. The male (inset, bottom) has a black hood and chestnut underparts. The female (inset, top) is olive above and yellow below with dusky wings.

Year-round | Adult male

HOUSE FINCH

Carpodacus mexicanus L 6" (15 cm)

FIELD MARKS

Male's forehead, bib, and rump are typically red, but can be orange or, occasionally, yellow

Brown streaked back, pale belly, streaked flanks

Female streaked dusky brown on entire body

Behavior

Forages on the ground in fields and suburban yards primarily for seeds, sometimes for insects or fruit. Often visits backyard feeders. Seen in large mixed-species flocks during winter. Flies in undulating pattern, during which squared-off tail is evident. Builds cup-like nest on buildings, in shrubs or trees, or on the ground. Male sings a lively, high-pitched song consisting of varied three-note phrases, usually ending in a nasal *wheeer*. Most common call is a whistled *wheat*.

Habitat

Adaptable to varied habitats, these birds are found abundantly in shrubby areas near human habitation, including urban and suburban parks.

Local Sites

Ubiquitous breeders in every habitat, including densely populated urban areas, House Finches are among the most common visitors to backyard feeders.

FIELD NOTES The Purple Finch, *Carpodacus purpureus,* is not purple but rose-red on the body of the adult male (inset, bottom). The female (inset, top) is gray-brown above and heavily streaked below, with a bolder face pattern and a more deeply notched tail than the House Finch. Look for both species in winter at bird feeding stations throughout the state.

Breeding | Adult male

AMERICAN GOLDFINCH

Carduelis tristis L 5" (13 cm)

FIELD MARKS
Breeding male is bright yellow with black cap; female and winter male duller overall, lacking cap

Black wings with white bars

Black-and-white tail; white undertail coverts

Behavior
Gregarious and active. Large winter flocks may include several other species. Typical goldfinch diet, mostly seeds, is the most vegetarian of any North American bird, though the goldfinch does sometimes eat insects as well. During courtship, male performs exaggerated, undulating aer-ial maneuvers, and often feeds the incubating female. Nests at forest edges or in old fields, often late in summer after thistles have bloomed so they can be used as nest lining and seeds as food for young. Song is a lively series of trills, twitters, and *swee* notes. Calls include a distinctive *per-chik-o-ree*, and a descending *ti-di-di-di*, given mainly in flight.

Habitat
Found in weedy fields, open woodlands, and anywhere rich in thistles and sunflowers.

Local Sites
These birds are common year-round in city parks, suburbs, and farm fields with scattered trees, everywhere in the state except the thickest forests.

FIELD NOTES The nonbreeding male goldfinch (inset) loses his black cap except for a spot just above the bill and molts into much drabber yellowish brown plumage. The nonbreeding female is similar, but an even drabber grayish overall.

Breeding | Adult male

HOUSE SPARROW

Passer domesticus L 6.3" (16 cm)

FIELD MARKS

Breeding male has black bill, bib, and lores; chestnut eye stripes, nape, back, and shoulders

Winter male less patterned

Female has brown back, streaked with black; buffy eyestripe; and unstreaked grayish breast

Behavior

Abundant and gregarious. Hops around, feeding on grain, seeds, and shoots, or seeks out bird feeders for sunflower seeds and millet. In urban areas, begs for food from humans and will clean up any crumbs left behind. In spring and summer, multiple suitors will chase a possible mate in high-speed aerial pursuit. Females choose mate mostly according to song display. Nests in any sheltered cavity; often usurping it, then vigorously defending it, from other species. Singing males give persistent *chirp* notes. Calls are variable.

Habitat

Found in close proximity to humans. Can be seen in urban and suburban areas and in rural landscapes inhabited by humans and livestock.

Local Sites

From big-city streets to isolated farms, these abundant breeders are found everywhere except in the heavily forested mountains.

FIELD NOTES Also known as the English Sparrow, the House Sparrow was first introduced into New York City in 1851 in an effort control insect pests. It has since spread across the continent to become one of the most successful bird species in North America, to the detriment of many native species. Ironically, its numbers are declining precipitously in its native England.

Color categories reflect the over-all colors of a species, not just the head color. Where sexes or ages differ, we typically show the most colorful plumage.

Mostly Black

 Double-crested Cormorant, 55

Turkey Vulture, 63

American Coot, 83

Chimney Swift, 117

American Crow, 147

Common Raven, 149

European Starling, 191

American Redstart, 213

Red-winged Blackbird, 247

Common Grackle, 251

Brown-headed Cowbird, 253

Mostly Black and White

Canvasback, 31

Ring-necked Duck, 33

Lesser Scaup, 35

 Bufflehead, 37

 Common Goldeneye, 39

 Hooded Merganser, 41

 Great Black-backed Gull, 99

 Red-bellied Woodpecker, 123

 Yellow-bellied Sapsucker, 125

 Downy Woodpecker, 127

 Pileated Woodpecker, 131

 Eastern Kingbird, 137

 Black-capped Chickadee, 161

 Chestnut-sided Warbler, 199

 Black-and-white Warbler, 211

 Eastern Towhee, 225

 Rose-breasted Grosbeak, 241

 Bobolink, 245

Mostly Blue

 Belted Kingfisher, 121

 Blue Jay, 145

 Purple Martin, 153

Tree Swallow, 155

Barn Swallow, 159

Eastern Bluebird, 177

 Northern Parula, 197

 Black-throated Blue Warbler, 205

Indigo Bunting, 243

Mostly Brown

American Black Duck, 23

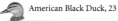 Green-winged Teal, 27

 Ring-necked Pheasant, 45

Ruffed Grouse, 47

Wild Turkey, 49

Pied-billed Grebe, 53

Red-shouldered Hawk, 73

Broad-winged Hawk, 75

American Kestrel, 79

American Woodcock, 93

 Eastern Screech-Owl, 111

 Great Horned Owl, 113

 Northern Flicker, 129

 Great Crested Flycatcher, 135

 Northern Rough-winged Swallow, 157

 Carolina Wren, 169

 House Wren, 171

 Veery, 179

 American Robin, 183

 Cedar Waxwing, 193

 Field Sparrow, 229

 House Sparrow, 261

Mostly Brown and White

 Canada Goose, 17

 Osprey, 65

 Bald Eagle, 67

Red-tailed Hawk, 77

 Killdeer, 85

Spotted Sandpiper, 89

Yellow-billed Cuckoo, 107

Barn Owl, 109

Horned Lark, 151

Brown Creeper, 167

Wood Thrush, 181

Brown Thrasher, 189

Ovenbird, 215

Louisiana Waterthrush, 217

Chipping Sparrow, 227

Savannah Sparrow, 231

Song Sparrow, 233

White-throated Sparrow, 235

Mostly Gray

Northern Pintail, 29

Common Loon, 50

Great Blue Heron, 59

Green Heron, 61

Northern Harrier, 69

Cooper's Hawk, 71

Peregrine Falcon, 81

Greater Yellowlegs, 87

Least Sandpiper, 91

Rock Pigeon, 103

Mourning Dove, 105

Common Nighthawk, 115

Eastern Phoebe, 133

Blue-headed Vireo, 141

Tufted Titmouse, 163

White-breasted Nuthatch, 165

Blue-gray Gnatcatcher, 175

Gray Catbird, 185

Northern Mockingbird, 187

Dark-eyed Junco, 237

Mostly Red

Scarlet Tanager, 223

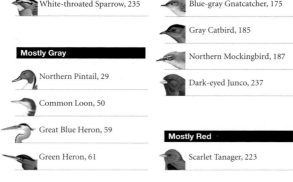

Northern Cardinal, 239

 House Finch, 257

Prominent Orange

 Blackburnian Warbler, 209

 Baltimore Oriole, 255

Mostly White

 Snow Goose, 15

 Tundra Swan, 19

 Great Egret, 59

 Bonaparte's Gull, 94

 Ring-billed Gull, 97

 Caspian Tern, 101

Prominent Yellow

 White-eyed Vireo, 139

 Blue-winged Warbler, 195

 Yellow Warbler, 201

 Magnolia Warbler, 203

 Black-throated Green Warbler, 207

 Common Yellowthroat, 219

 Hooded Warbler, 221

 Eastern Meadowlark, 249

 American Goldfinch, 259

Mostly Greenish

 Ruby-throated Hummingbird, 119

 Red-eyed Vireo, 143

 Golden-crowned Kinglet, 173

Prominent Green Head

 Wood Duck, 21

 Mallard, 25

 Common Merganser, 43

The first entry page number for each species is listed in **boldface** type and refers to the text page opposite the illustration.

A check-off box is provided next to each common-name entry so that you can use this index as a checklist of the species you have identified.

Blackbird
❏ Red-winged **247**
Bluebird
❏ Eastern **177**
❏ Bobolink **245**
❏ Bufflehead **37**
Bunting
❏ Indigo **243**

❏ **C**anvasback **31**
Cardinal
☒ Northern **239**
❏ Catbird, Gray **185**
❏ Chat, Yellow-breasted **219**
Chickadee
☒ Black-capped **161**
❏ Carolina 161
Coot
❏ American **83**
Cormorant
☒ Double-crested **55**
Cowbird
☒ Brown-headed **253**
❏ Creeper, Brown **167**
Crow
❏ American **147**
❏ Fish 147
Cuckoo
❏ Black-billed **107**
❏ Yellow-billed **107**

Dove
❏ Mourning **105**
Duck
❏ American Black **23**
❏ Ring-necked **33**
❏ Wood **21**

Eagle
❏ Bald **67**
Egret
❏ Great **59**

Falcon
❏ Peregrine **81**
Finch
❏ House **257**
❏ Purple **257**
Flicker
❏ Northern **37**, **129**
Flycatcher
❏ Great Crested **135**

Gnatcatcher
❏ Blue-gray **175**
Goldeneye
❏ Common **39**
Goldfinch
☒ American **259**
Goose
☒ Cackling **17**
❏ Canada **17**
❏ Snow **15**
Grackle
❏ Common **251**
Grebe
❏ Horned **53**
❏ Pied-billed **53**
Grosbeak
❏ Rose-breasted **241**
Grouse
❏ Ruffed **47**

Gull
- ❑ Bonaparte's **95**
- ❑ Great Black-backed **99**
- ❑ Herring **97**
- ❑ Lesser Black-backed **99**
- ❑ Ring-billed **97**

Harrier
- ❑ Northern **69**

Hawk
- ❑ Broad-winged **75**
- ❑ Cooper's **71**
- ❑ Red-shouldered **73**
- ❑ Red-tailed **77**
- ❑ Sharp-shinned **71**

Heron
- ❑ Black-crowned Night- **57**
- ❑ Great Blue **57**
- ❑ Green **61**

Hummingbird
- ❑ Ruby-throated **119**

Jay
- ☒ Blue **145**

Junco
- ❑ Dark-eyed **237**

Kestrel
- ❑ American **79**
- ☑ Killdeer **85**

Kingbird
- ❑ Eastern **137**

Kingfisher
- ❑ Belted **121**

Kinglet
- ❑ Golden-crowned **173**
- ❑ Ruby-crowned 173

Lark
- ❑ Horned **151**

Loon

- ❑ Common **51**
- ❑ Red-throated 51

❑ **M**allard 23, **25**

Martin
- ❑ Purple **153**

Meadowlark
- ❑ Eastern **249**

Merganser
- ❑ Common **43**
- ❑ Hooded **41**
- ❑ Red-breasted 43

❑ Merlin **81**

Mockingbird
- ❑ Northern **187**

❑ Moorhen, Common **83**

Nighthawk
- ❑ Common **115**

Nuthatch
- ❑ Red-breasted 165
- ❑ White-breasted **165**

Oriole
- ❑ Baltimore **255**
- ❑ Orchard **255**

❑ Osprey **65**

❑ Ovenbird **215**

Owl
- ❑ Barn **109**
- ❑ Barred 113
- ❑ Eastern Screech- **111**
- ❑ Great Horned **113**
- ❑ Northern Saw-whet 111

Parula
- ❑ Northern **197**

Pewee
- ❑ Eastern Wood- 133

❑ Pheasant, Ring-necked **45**

Phoebe

Eastern **133**
Pigeon
Rock **103**
Pintail
Northern 27

Raven
Common **149**
Redhead 31
Redstart
American **213**
Robin
American **183**

Sandpiper
Least **91**
Semipalmated 91
Solitary 89
Spotted **89**
Sapsucker
Yellow-bellied **125**
Scaup
Greater **35**
Lesser **35**
Shoveler
Northern 25
Snipe
Wilson's 93
Sparrow
American Tree 227
Chipping **227**
Field **229**
Fox **231**
House **261**
Savannah **231**
Song **233**
Swamp **233**
White-crowned **235**
White-throated **235**
Starling, European **191**
Swallow

Bank 157
Barn **159**
Cliff 159
Northern Rough-winged 157
Tree **155**
Swan
Mute 19
Tundra **19**
Swift
Chimney **117**

Tanager
Scarlet **223**
Teal
Green-winged **29**
Tern
Caspian **101**
Common **101**
Thrasher
Brown **189**
Thrush
Hermit **181**
Wood **181**
Titmouse
Tufted **163**
Towhee
Eastern **225**
Turkey, Wild **49**

Veery **179**
Vireo
Blue-headed **141**
Red-eyed **143**
Warbling 143
White-eyed **139**
Yellow-throated 139
Vulture
Black 63
Turkey **63**

Warbler
- ❏ Black-and-white **211**
- ❏ Black-throated Blue **205**
- ❏ Black-throated Green **207**
- ❏ Blackburnian **209**
- ❏ Blue-winged **195**
- ❏ Cerulean 205
- ❏ Chestnut-sided **199**
- ❏ Golden-winged 195
- ❏ Hooded **221**
- ❏ Kentucky 221
- ❏ Magnolia **203**
- ❏ Nashville 197
- ❏ Prairie 201
- ❏ Yellow **201**
- ❏ Yellow-rumped 203
- ❏ Yellow-throated 211

Waterthrush
- ❏ Louisiana **217**
- ❏ Northern 217

Waxwing
- ❏ Cedar **193**
- ❏ Whip-poor-will 115

Woodcock
- ❏ American **93**

Woodpecker
- ❏ Downy **127**
- ❏ Hairy 127
- ❏ Pileated **131**
- ☑ Red-bellied **123**
- ❏ Red-headed 123

Wren
- ❏ Carolina **169**
- ❏ House **171**
- ❏ Winter 171

Yellowlegs
- ❏ Greater **87**
- ❏ Lesser 87

Yellowthroat
- ❏ Common **219**

ACKNOWLEDGMENTS

The Book Division would like to thank the following people for their guidance and contribution in creating the *National Geographic Field Guide to Birds: Pennsylvania*.

Cortez C. Austin, Jr.:
Cortez Austin is a wildlife photographer specializing in North American and tropical birds. An ardent conservationist, he has donated images, given lectures, and written book reviews for conservation organizations. In addition he has published numerous articles and photographs in birding magazines. His photographs have also appeared in field guides and wildlife books.

Richard Crossley:
Richard Crossley is an Englishman obsessed by birding since age 10. He traveled the world studying birds but fell in love with Cape May while pioneering the identification of overhead warbler migration in 1985. He is co-author of *The Shorebird Guide*, due in Spring 2006.

Bates Littlehales:
National Geographic photographer for more than 30 years covering myriad subjects around the globe, Bates Littlehales continues to specialize in photographing birds and is an expert in capturing their beauty and ephemeral nature. Bates is co-author of the *National Geographic Photographic Field Guide: Birds*, and a contributor to the *National Geographic Reference Atlas to the Birds of North America*.

Brian E. Small:
Brian E. Small has been a full-time professional wildlife photographer specializing in birds for more than 15 years. In addition, he has been a regular columnist and Advisory Board member for *WildBird* magazine for the past 10 years. An avid naturalist and enthusiastic birder, Brian is currently the Photo Editor for the American Birding Association's *Birding* magazine. You can find more of his images at www.briansmallphoto.com.

Tom Vezo:
Tom Vezo is an award-winning wildlife photographer who is widely published throughout the U.S. and Europe. He specializes in bird photography but photographs other wildlife and nature subjects as well. He is a contributor to the *National Geographic Reference Atlas to the Birds of North America*. Please visit Tom at his website www.tomvezo.com.

Cortez C. Austin, Jr.: pp. 16, 20, 36, 42, 54, 56, 84, 158, 192, 250. **Tom Brakefield/CORBIS:** p. 46. **Richard Crossley:** pp. 92, 182. **Mike Danzenbaker:** p. 116. **Bates Littlehales:** pp. 112, 208, 212, 218, 224. **Larry Sansone:** p. 148. **Rulon E. Simmons:** p. 64. **Brian E. Small:** pp. Cover, 30, 32, 34, 38, 40, 58, 62, 66, 72, 88, 90, 102, 104, 106, 114, 120, 138, 140, 142, 150, 156, 166, 168, 176, 178, 180, 186, 188, 190, 194, 202, 204, 206, 210, 216, 226, 230, 232, 234, 238, 260. **Bob Steele:** pp. 2, 68. **TomVezo.com:** pp. 14, 18, 22, 24, 26, 28, 44, 48, 50, 52, 60, 70, 74, 76, 78, 80, 82, 86, 94, 96, 98, 100, 108, 110, 122, 124, 126, 128, 130, 132, 134, 136, 144, 146, 152, 154, 160, 162, 164, 170, 172, 174, 184, 196, 200, 214, 220, 228, 236, 240, 242, 246, 248, 252, 254, 256, 258, 262. **Garth McElroy/VIREO:** p. 198. **Rob & Ann Simpson/VIREO:** p. 222. **T.J. Ulrich/VIREO:** p. 118.

NATIONAL GEOGRAPHIC
FIELD GUIDE TO BIRDS:
PENNSYLVANIA

Edited by Jonathan Alderfer

**Published by
the National Geographic Society**

John M. Fahey, Jr.,
President and Chief Executive Officer

Gilbert M. Grosvenor,
Chairman of the Board

Nina D. Hoffman,
*Executive Vice President;
President, Books & School Publishing*

Prepared by the Book Division

Kevin Mulroy,
Senior Vice President and Publisher

Kristin Hanneman, *Illustrations Director*

Marianne R. Koszorus, *Design Director*

Carl Mehler, *Director of Maps*

Barbara Brownell Grogan,
Executive Editor

Staff for this Book

Barbara Levitt, *Editor*

Kate Griffin, *Illustrations Editor*

Alexandra Littlehales, *Designer*

Carol Norton, *Series Art Director*

Suzanne Poole, *Text Editor*

Teresa Tate, *Illustrations Specialist*

Paul Hess, *Map Researcher*

Matt Chwastyk, Sven M. Dolling,
Map Production

Lauren Pruneski, Michael Greninger,
Editorial Assistants

Rick Wain, *Production Project Manager*

Manufacturing and Quality Control

Christopher A. Liedel,
Chief Financial Officer

Phillip L. Schlosser, *Managing Director*

One of the world's largest nonprofit
scientific and educational organizations,
the National Geographic Society was
founded in 1888 "for the increase and
diffusion of geographic knowledge."
Fulfilling this mission, the Society edu-
cates and inspires millions every day
through its magazines, books, television
programs, videos, maps and atlases,
research grants, the National Geographic
Bee, teacher workshops, and innovative
classroom materials. The Society is sup-
ported through membership dues, chari-
table gifts, and income from the sale of
its educational products. This support is
vital to National Geographic's mission to
increase global understanding and pro-
mote conservation of our planet through
exploration, research, and education.

For more information, please call
1-800-NGS LINE (647-5463) or write
to the following address:

National Geographic Society
1145 17th Street N.W.
Washington, D.C. 20036-4688 U.S.A.

Visit the Society's Web site at
www.nationalgeographic.com.

**Library of Congress
Cataloging-in-Publication Data**

Available upon request.